Present Perfect

Finding God in the Now

Gregory A. Boyd

Bestselling Author of *The Myth of a Christian Nation*

ZONDERVAN®

ZONDERVAN.com/
AUTHORTRACKER
follow your favorite authors

ZONDERVAN

Present Perfect
Copyright © 2010 by Gregory A. Boyd

This title is also available as a Zondervan ebook.
Visit www.zondervan.com/ebooks.

This title is also available in a Zondervan audio edition.
Visit www.zondervan.fm.

Requests for information should be addressed to:
Zondervan, *Grand Rapids, Michigan* 49530

Library of Congress Cataloging-in-Publication Data

Boyd, Gregory A., 1957-
    Present perfect : discovering God's kingdom in the now / Gregory A. Boyd.
        p.   cm.
    Includes bibliographical references (p. 163)
    ISBN 978-0-310-28384-3 (softcover)
    1. Spiritual life—Christianity. I. Title.
    BV4501.3.B693   2010
    248.4—dc22   2010001878

All Scripture quotations, unless otherwise indicated, are taken from the Holy Bible,
New International Version®, NIV®. Copyright © 1973, 1978, 1984 by Biblica, Inc.™ Used
by permission of Zondervan. All rights reserved worldwide.

The song "Time" by Roger Waters is used by permission of Hampshire House Publishing. All rights reserved.

Cover design: Jeff Gifford
Cover photography: Veer
Interior design: Michelle Espinoza

Printed in the United States of America

10 11 12 13 14 15 /DCI/ 21 20 19 18 17 16 15 14 13 12 11 10 9 8 7 6 5 4 3 2 1

Greg has landed on a topic as ancient as time and as timely as this moment. To live in both ways is to find life itself!

JOHN ORTBERG, author and pastor, Menlo Park Presbyterian Church

Greg Boyd has a marvelous knack for sensing what is essential for the times in which we live. If faith involves coming to attention, then *Present Perfect* sounds like a needed clarion call in our profoundly distracted culture. Drawing deeply from the great guides in Scripture and history, Greg helps us to see God *everywhere* and to engage him more fully *anytime*. Get into it.

ALAN HIRSCH, author of *The Forgotten Ways* and coauthor of *Untamed*, (www.theforgottenways.org)

When people ask what has been the single most important personal discipline in my own spiritual life, I always point them toward something I learned from an old classic back in my college years: practicing God's presence. But I've never had a readable contemporary book to recommend that would make this practice more widely accessible to people today, until now. Greg Boyd's book will help a new generation of readers discover a spiritual secret that is as simple as it is profound, as transformative as it is within anyone's reach. Highly recommended.

BRIAN D. MCLAREN, author/speaker/activist (brianmclaren.net)

A dazzling reminder that the Christian life is not just about going up when we die, but about bringing God's kingdom down. Brother Greg offers a fiery and thoughtful invitation to see that eternity begins now and that Jesus did not simply come to prepare us to die, but to teach us to live. Read it, and hear the invitation to join God's little infection of grace and goodness that is spreading across the globe.

SHANE CLAIBORNE, author, activist, and recovering sinner (www.thesimpleway.org)

Greg Boyd has already proven himself to be a voice of conscience in the evangelical church. Now, with *Present Perfect*, he will become a voice of sound spiritual wisdom. By (re)introducing the idea of constant awareness of God, Boyd challenges each of us to develop a Christ-consciousness. This book should be on the shelf of anyone who wants to have a deeper prayer life.

TONY JONES, author of *The Sacred Way: Spiritual Practices for Everyday Life*, (tonyj.net)

Also by Gregory A. Boyd

The Myth of a Christian Nation
The Myth of the Christian Religion

This book is dedicated to
my precious son,
Nathan,
my wonderful daughters,
Denay and Alisha,
my two outstanding sons-in-law,
Heighlos and Tim,
and my two unbelievably adorable grandchildren,
Soel and Sage.
Shelley and I love all of you
more than words could possibly convey

Contents

Introduction: *"Now" Is Where God Lives*   9

1. Mere Christianity   27

2. Finding Home   43

3. Chasing the Sun   59

4. Single-Mindedness   83

5. Living in Love   97

6. Being Present   115

7. The Father Is Always Working   131

Conclusion: Firstfruits   149

Appendix: Practicing the Presence and the New Age Movement   153

Acknowledgments   161

Notes   163

"Now" Is Where God Lives

Can I bring the Lord back into my mind-flow
every few seconds
so that God shall always be in my mind?
I choose to make the rest of my life
an experiment
in answering this question.

Frank Laubach[1]

Ever-present Abba,
you uphold all things
by the power of your Word
and your love surrounds us
every moment
of every day.
Help us to remember you
in this moment
and in every moment.

Are You Awake?

The surest sign that you're awake is that you're aware of your surroundings. The surest sign that you're asleep is that you're not.

The present moment is all that matters.

J.-P. de Caussade

If God is present in all places at all times, which is what the Bible teaches, then God is part of our surroundings each and every moment — or as the apostle Paul says, "In him we live and move and have our being" (Acts 17:28). The question is, Are you aware of God surrounding you? Are you awake or asleep to God's presence?

This book was written to help you stay awake to God's presence and discover for yourself why this is the most important discipline you could ever practice.

But don't wait till you finish this book — or even read another sentence — before you wake up! The only thing that's real is this present moment, and the only thing that matters is waking up to God's presence — now. I encourage you to become aware of God's presence all around you. As you read this sentence, be aware that God is closer to you than the air you breathe.

Don't try to *feel* his presence. In fact, don't try to *do* anything at all. Simply be mindful of the fact that you are, in this present moment, submerged in the ocean of God's perfect love.

Some people have compared [remaining aware of God's presence] to getting out of a dark prison and beginning to live. We still see the same world, yet it is not the same, for it has a new, glorious color and a far deeper meaning.

Frank Laubach

Right now, stop reading for a second and just breathe in God's presence as you take your next couple breaths. Then, as you continue to read, see how often you can remind yourself of that fact. How awake can you remain?

Waking Up to a Cricket

I used to run in ultramarathons (ranging from 50 to 100 miles) — don't ask me why. To train, I'd occasionally go on three- to six-hour runs through the woods.

One fall morning, as I ran my laps on a beautiful five-mile trail that circled a lake, I prayed and enjoyed the scenery, though my mind was mostly focused on an upcoming race. I wondered whether I could win and what my strategy should be. I thought about what had and hadn't worked in previous races, and I worried that perhaps I hadn't trained enough. I wondered if the soreness in my left Achilles' tendon would improve or worsen—all the sort of things runners typically obsess about.

About two hours into my run, however, something unusual happened. I noticed a cricket chirping. For reasons that still escape me, I slowed down to pay closer attention. Immediately I noticed another cricket, then another. In a moment I was surrounded by a choir of crickets! It seemed to me they had just started singing, though I knew this couldn't be true. They had to have been chirping throughout my run—but I just hadn't been listening. As I came to a halt, I giggled in amazement at how deaf I'd been.

Then something else remarkable occurred. As I stood in the middle of the trail, my ears opened up to an explosion of sounds—marvelous sounds. It seemed as though a million frogs were croaking their hearts out in the lake. They were so loud! How had I *not* noticed them before? A dozen or so bees hummed gently as they flittered in and out of a flowerbed in front of me.

Each moment is a revelation of God.

J.-P. de Caussade

Distant grasshoppers contributed an odd, random buzzing. A magnificent, diverse choir of birds was proclaiming the wonders of creation. It was stunning. How had I missed all this until now?

My eyes also opened. I became aware of magical streaks of light from the new morning sun piercing the foliage overhead. A light mist hovered on the surface of the water. A swarm of gnats danced in the morning sun just off shore,

and farther out on the lake, veiled in the mist, I spotted a
family of geese. A nearby hummingbird darted in and out
of radiant red and yellow flowers. A squirrel raced across an
overhead branch. A couple of dragonflies danced with each
other on a nearby plant. Gazing down, I noticed an ant car-
rying a leaf at least twenty times its
size, and in that moment it seemed
I'd never seen anything quite so
amazing! I quickly became aware
that this little fellow was just part
of an entire civilization of insects
that were scurrying about, busy

> It is not pleasure we
> seek. Let this exercise [of
> practicing God's presence]
> be done from one motive
> alone: because we love him.
>
> Brother Lawrence

with their various tasks on the edge of the trail. How had I
been blind to all this living art before now?

My sense of smell came alive as well. I became acutely
aware that I was breathing in a spectacular array of fra-
grances. Flowers, leaves, bark, morning dew, the lake—
what a feast! I had smelled all these before, of course, but
never like this!

The moment felt sacred. I felt I was waking up to God's
presence permeating all things and reflected in all things.
It seemed I was, for the first time, waking up to the way the
world is supposed to be experienced—the way it really *is*.
Overwhelmed by this sense of God's presence and breath-
taking beauty, I began to weep.

Now Is Where God Lives

I'm not sure how long the experience lasted, for I wasn't aware of the passage of time. But at some point the wonder began to fade, and my awareness of the world returned to "normal." For a little while I tried to recover the sense of wonder, like a person wanting to return to a dream they don't want to wake up from. But it was no use. Yet when I resumed running I did so with a new awareness that has profoundly affected my life ever since.

I realized that my trivial, self-centered mental chatter about the past and future—like a dark cloud blocking the sun—had kept me from seeing the glory of God that surrounded me every second of every day. Never before had I realized the extent to which our focus determines what we experience—and do not experience—in any given moment. Never before had I seen how being absorbed in the past or future causes us to miss the wonder of the present. This realization began to move me toward what I've since come to believe is the most fundamental truth a person can ever embrace, and it's the truth this book is all about.

The present moment is *all* that is real.

Are you awake?

The past is gone. The future is not yet. We remember the past and anticipate the future, but we always do so *in the present*. Reality is always *now*. And the single most important aspect of reality is that God is present in it every moment. To forget that God is present in any given moment is to forget the most important aspect of that moment.

God is the God of the living, not the God of the already-past or the not-yet-present. He's the great "I AM," not the great "I was" or the great "I will be." He's been present in every moment in the past, for which we can be thankful, and he'll be present at every moment in the future, which gives us great hope. But he's *only* alive and active now, in the present — which is, once again, the only thing that's real.

Experiences like mine in the woods are rare; they are divine gifts. We can't make them happen and we shouldn't try. But the kind of acute awareness of God's presence that I had on that fall morning should *not* be rare. On the contrary, I believe such awareness is to be the norm for every lover of God. What matters is not profound spiritual experiences, though we thank God when they occur. What matters is that we remain awake to God's ever-present reality every moment, however trivial these moments might otherwise seem.

> *My set times for prayer are exactly like the rest of the day to me. They are but a continuation of the same exercise of being in God's presence.*
>
> Brother Lawrence

Over the past twenty-plus years since my waking-up experience in the woods, I've become absolutely convinced that remaining aware of God's presence is the single most important task in the life of every follower of Jesus. I'm

convinced this challenge is implied in our commitment to
surrender our life to Christ, for the only real life we have to
surrender to him is the one we
live each moment.

I will devote myself exclusively to
the duty of the present moment to
love you, to fulfill my obligations
and to let your will be done.

It is my prayer that God
will use this book to help you
wake up to his ever-present
love and to passionately em-
brace the challenge of remaining awake to this love as the
central goal of your life.

J.-P. de Caussade

Practicing the Presence of God

Since that morning in the woods I have come across
a number of writers who have helped me appreciate the
importance of remaining aware of God's presence and who
have helped me grow in my ability to do this. Three such
writers in the Christian tradition stand head and shoul-
ders above the rest and are the primary inspiration for this
book.

Shortly after my experience I discovered a little book
entitled *Practicing the Presence of God* by a humble seventeenth-century monk named Brother Lawrence. Among
the many things I learned from this man was the need to
stop thinking of prayer as something we do at certain times
but not others. Brother Lawrence encourages us to abolish
the distinction between special times devoted to prayer and
worship on the one hand, and "ordinary" times when God

is mostly excluded from our awareness on the other. Rather, he encourages us to aspire to transform every moment of our life into an act of prayer and worship. For more than twenty years he was a dishwasher in a monastery (a job he deplored), but he found that this mundane task became a joy-filled holy sacrament when he consciously offered up his labor to God moment-by-moment.

Later I came upon the writings of another little-known seventeenth-century monk named Jean-Pierre de Caussade who espoused a similar practice, sometimes referring to it as "our duty to the present moment" or "the sacrament of this present moment." In some respects, this fiery priest goes beyond Brother Lawrence in emphasizing our need to surrender to God's presence every moment. To remain aware of that presence implies yielding to God's will.

Whatever else may be going on in our lives, the ultimate goal must be to consciously obey what one senses God's will to be. To "seek first the kingdom of God," as Jesus commanded, we must first seek to submit to God's reign in each and every moment. When we do this, de Caussade proclaims, we transform ordinary moments into sacred moments, and our life becomes a living sacrament. He and millions of others have discovered that this continual

Can we have that contact with God all the time? All the time awake, fall asleep in His arms, and awaken in His presence? Can we attain that? Can we do His will all the time? Can we think His thoughts all the time?

Frank Laubach

submission is the key to experiencing the fullness of God's love, joy, and peace.

Recently I've become familiar with the reflections of Frank Laubach, a twentieth-century missionary to the Philippines who offers insights derived from his own experience of struggling to remain perpetually aware of (and, therefore, yielded to) God's presence. In 1930 this remarkable man dedicated his whole life to answering one simple question: Is it possible to remain aware of God's presence every waking moment? In his writings Laubach encourages us to make our lives an ongoing experiment in answering this question. He beautifully describes the love, joy, and transformation he experienced as he learned to remain awake to God's presence. I've found his reflections to be inspiring, encouraging, and extremely helpful as I've endeavored to practice the presence of God in my own life.

> The practice [of God's presence] is so simple, so easy and so accessible that it need only be wished for it to be had.
>
> J.-P. de Caussade

While these three authors differ widely in both their theology and their emphasis, they all emphatically agree that remaining awake to God's presence in the present moment is the single most important task of the Christian life and that no spiritual discipline is more foundational or transforming than this one.

I've been a Christian for thirty-four years now, during which time I've read close to a hundred books about the spiritual disciplines and attended numerous conferences on the subject. I've gained a lot of valuable insight from these sources. But like these three authors, I have found the simple practice of remaining aware of God's presence each moment brings me to the point toward which all other disciplines aspire. It is, I'm convinced, the bedrock of a vibrant relationship with God and the key to transformation into the likeness of Christ.

> *I kept my mind in His holy presence. I recalled His presence as often as I found my mind wandering from Him. I found this to be a very difficult exercise! Yet I continued despite the difficulties I encountered. I did not allow myself to become upset when my mind wandered.*
>
> Brother Lawrence

The Simplicity and Challenge of Practicing the Presence

Lawrence, de Caussade, and Laubach all proclaim that no spiritual discipline is easier or more accessible to everyone than this one, for waking up to God's presence requires nothing more than remembering God's presence each moment. Right now, as you read this sentence, remind yourself that you are submerged in God's love. *That* is the practice of the presence of God. Could anything be easier?

At the same time, no spiritual discipline could be more challenging. The challenge is not in *doing* the discipline: it's in *remembering* the discipline.

A moment ago you discovered how easy it is to become aware of God's presence in a given moment. But now honestly ask yourself, Have I remained aware of God's presence as I read these few sentences since I engaged in that simple exercise?

Your answer, of course, doesn't matter because that's now in the past, and the only thing that is real and that matters is *this* present moment. So right now remind yourself once again that you are in the presence of God.

Now see if you can retain God in your awareness as you read the next several sentences.

When you notice that you've forgotten God, don't get frustrated or angry. This only produces more mental chatter, which keeps you still further from living in the present. It's vital that we don't "keep score" on how we're doing and turn this into a contest with ourselves or others. Nor should this ever become a laborious task we engage in, thinking it somehow earns God's love. Such attitudes only intensify our focus on ourselves and keep us obsessed with the past ("How did I do?") and the future ("Will I be able to sustain this?"). Instead, embrace this discipline as a way of being liberated from the prison of our self-preoccupation while waking up to the beauty and joy of God.

So when you realize you've gone a long while without remembering God, simply remind yourself that the only thing that is real — and the only thing that matters — is *this*

present moment. *Now* is where God lives. Calmly let go of the past and, as Laubach says, "Make a fresh beginning." Wake up to God's presence in this moment *now*.

Now stay awake to God's presence in this one.

Many who embark on this discipline find it helpful to post strategic reminders around their house, in the car, in the office, and so on. I even put reminders in my sermon notes, for (ironically enough) I find preaching to be one of the hardest times to stay awake to God's presence. That's probably because when I have a couple thousand people staring at me, my mind tends to get preoccupied with questions like: Is my point getting across? Where am I in my notes? What point comes next? Am I talking too fast? How much time do I have left? So, at least once or twice on every page of my sermon notes, I write in bold letters: **Are you awake?**

These reminders not only help me remember God's presence while I preach, but they also help me preach better. Staying conscious of God's presence means I have to relinquish a bit of control, which my fallen mind resists doing. Part of me fears that if I don't invest every ounce of consciousness into staying "on task," I'll forget a point or lose my place. But I've found that if I can simply relinquish this need to control

> *If you should forget Him for minutes or even days, do not groan or repent, but begin anew with a smile. Every minute can be a fresh beginning.*
>
> Frank Laubach

and consecrate part of my awareness to remembering God is with me, my sermons actually tend to go better.

Lawrence, de Caussade, and Laubach each testify that whatever task occupies you at any given moment, you'll tend to do it better if you include God. Remaining aware of God's presence doesn't compete with our attention to other things; it augments it.

This practicing the presence of Christ takes all our time, yet does not take from our work. It takes Christ into our enterprises and makes them more successful.

Frank Laubach

And this applies to reading this book. What more appropriate place to practice the presence of God than in a book on the topic? To help you, therefore, I've placed little *"Are you awake?"* reminders throughout the text, just as I do my sermon notes. When you come upon these, I encourage you to pause, remind yourself you are in the presence of Almighty God, and then continue reading—trying not to fall back asleep to his presence as you do so.

About This Book

While this book was inspired by Brother Lawrence, Jean-Pierre de Caussade, and Frank Laubach, it's not about those authors (though I hope you'll be inspired to seek out these three authors for yourself). I make no effort to analyze their teachings, study their historical context, or resolve differing interpretations. Nor do I discuss their different theological views. Instead, this book is a collection of reflections

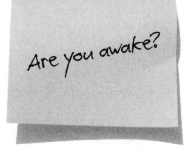
Are you awake?

that express why I believe
this practice is founda-
tional to Christianity and
how this practice can transform our lives. This book also
offers practical advice in staying awake.

First, however, I must make a confession. After several
months of making the practice of the presence of God the
all-consuming goal of his life, Frank Laubach testified that
he had a remarkable breakthrough, after which he found the
practice to be relatively easy. It became natural for him consciously to include God in everything he thought and did.
Brother Lawrence and Jean-Pierre de Caussade as well as
others throughout history seem to have had similar experiences. After more than twenty years of this practice (admit-
tedly, with varying degrees of intensity), I confess that I've
had no such breakthrough. As magnificently rewarding and
transforming as I've found this discipline to be, I *still* find
remembering God's presence moment-by-moment to be
extremely challenging.

In fact, in the interest of full disclosure, I should admit
that I actually wrote a draft of this book over four years ago
at a time when I was rereading Lawrence, de Caussade,
and Laubach in order to rededicate myself to this practice
(after having slacked off for several years). I originally wrote
the essays in this book as a means of helping myself think
through the profound meaning and significance of this
practice. When I was done I thought others might find the

essays helpful, so I planned on submitting them for publication. At the last minute, however, I decided against it. Why? Because I felt like a hypocrite! How could I write a book about a practice that I myself hadn't come close to mastering?

I've improved my "holy habit" (as Brother Lawrence calls it) somewhat over the last four years, but not nearly enough to write this book from the perspective of a master. The truth is that I'm no Brother Lawrence! The reason I've changed my mind and decided to publish my reflections is that I now understand that one doesn't have to write from the perspective of a master to help others benefit from the masters.

In fact, I've come to realize that there's a certain advantage to writing as a fellow pilgrim instead of as a master. After twenty years of engaging in this discipline, I've had enough experience to know its profound significance and transforming power. Yet I'm still enough of a novice to fully appreciate the formidable challenges this discipline poses.

You may tell me that I am always saying the same thing. It is true, for this is the best and easiest method I know. In it is the resolution of all other spiritual problems.

Brother Lawrence

One final word: each of the following meditations reflect on the significance and power of practicing the presence from a slightly different angle. The word *meditation* implies looking at something from a variety of angles, as a jeweler might inspect a diamond. This is what

I'll be doing with this discipline. While some chapters build on others, readers should not expect a straightforward, linear, topical development. Each essay may be read and reflected on as though it stood alone. Moreover, since each chapter revolves around essentially the same topic, readers should expect a certain amount of overlap. I am not trying to give new information with each chapter as much as seeking to deepen our awareness of God's presence.

Because these essays are meditations, I encourage you to read them slowly and prayerfully, with a view toward how each one impacts your own spiritual transformation. I also strongly encourage you to engage in the exercises found at the end of each chapter. These are important if this book is to bring about transformation. The material in this book — and in any other book or seminar, for that matter — will remain mere information unless you are intentional about applying it to your life. Gathering new information is easy: translating it into transformation is the challenge.

The exercises flow out of my own experience and don't come close to exhausting the topic. I encourage you to be open to other spiritual exercises that better fit your personality or life-situation.[2] Moreover, don't expect every exercise to have equal value. What works for one person may have little effect on another. I encourage you to experiment with all the exercises but only integrate those that seem to work best for you.

Most likely you will find that your favorite exercises will

need to change over time as you grow and face new life situations. Exercises that were indispensable at one stage of life may become irrelevant at a different stage, while exercises that didn't seem to evoke much change earlier in life may suddenly take on new significance and power at a later stage of life. Never stop experimenting and growing.

Whatever exercises appeal to you, my prayer is that this book will motivate you to embrace the core discipline of practicing the presence of God as the central goal of your life. As multitudes throughout history can testify, no other single discipline has the power to revolutionize how we experience life moment-by-moment as the largely forgotten and profoundly simple discipline of remembering God exists, right here and right now.

God is *now*.

Chapter 1

Mere Christianity

So begin ...
make that resolution.
Now! ... Be daring.
None of us have a long time to live ...
what years we have,
let us live them with God.

Brother Lawrence

Our ever-present Father,
We pledged to surrender our life to you,
but we confess
that most of the moments that make up our actual life
are not surrendered to you.
Help us,
to remember you
and offer ourselves up to you
in this moment
and in every moment.

For the Supersaints Only?

When many Christians first hear about the practice of the presence of God, it strikes them as an impossible discipline. Perhaps supersaints locked up in monasteries can attain this level of awareness, but not us average folk who work nine-to-five jobs and raise families! It's hard enough to pray ten minutes a day and make it to church once a week! For us ordinary Christians, trying to remain aware of God's presence moment-by-moment seems like a hyperspiritual pipe dream.

If you're inclined to feel this way, it might be because, like everyone else in modern Western culture, you've been brainwashed by what is called "the secular worldview." In this view of the world, what's real, or at least what's important, is the physical here-and-now. When we're brainwashed by this worldview, we experience

the world as though God did not exist, for we habitually exclude him from our awareness. We may still *believe* in God, of course, but he's not *real* to us most of the time.

Because of this we go about our day-to-day lives as functional atheists. We may pray and worship God on occasion, but these are "special times," isolated from our "normal," secular day-to-day life. So thoroughly are we brainwashed by the secular mind-set that the very suggestion that we could routinely experience the world in a way that *includes* God strikes us as impossible.

If you're looking for an explanation why so few contemporary believers experience the fullness of love, joy, peace, and the transforming

> *I wish to make all see that everyone can aspire ... to the same love, the same surrender, the same God and his work, and thereby effortlessly achieve the most perfect saintliness.*
>
> J.-P. de Caussade

power that the New Testament promises, I think you've just found it. The secular worldview causes us to compartmentalize our life, isolating the "spiritual" from the rest of our experience. Our relationship with God is boxed into special prayer and devotion times along with weekend church services, all of which have little impact on us. But in the process of segregating God from our "normal" life, we block the love, joy, peace, and transforming power of God.

If we're ever going to experience the fullness of Life that the New Testament promises us, we're going to have to tear down the walls that compartmentalize the "spiritual" and "normal."[1] We're going to have to accept a new definition of "normal," and this means we need to get over our mistaken idea that the practice of the presence of God is only for the "superholy."

> God is only asking for your hearts. If you truly seek this treasure, this kingdom where God alone reigns, you will find it. Your heart, if it is totally surrendered to God, is itself that treasure, that very kingdom you long for and are seeking.
>
> J.-P. de Caussade

The call to practice the presence of God is not a hyperspiritual exercise. On the contrary, it's the core of what it means to surrender our life to Christ. Though few realize it, this practice is woven into the very fabric of the New Testament, written for *all* followers of Jesus. Aspiring to remain awake to God's ever-present love is simply an aspect — a foundational aspect — of what C. S. Lewis referred to as "mere Christianity."[2]

Living Out the Pledge of Life

We began our walk with God when we confessed our need for Jesus and pledged to surrender our life to him. But we often fail to notice that our pledge to surrender our life to Christ isn't itself the life we pledged to surrender. The life we pledged to surrender is the life we've lived each and every moment since we initially made the pledge to surrender our life. For the only life we have to surrender to Christ is the one we live moment-by-moment.

Think of it like a marriage. Thirty-one years ago I

looked into my wife's gorgeous eyes and pledged my life to her. But my pledge wasn't itself the life I pledged to her. My pledge didn't magically give us a good marriage (would that it were that simple!). Rather, the actual life I pledged to my wife was the life I have lived each and every moment since I made that pledge. The only life I have to give to my wife is the life I live moment-by-moment.

The quality of my marriage, therefore, isn't decided by whether I made a pledge thirty-one years ago. It's determined by how I live out that pledge *now*. The same is true of our relationship with Christ. The important question is not, Did I once surrender my life to Christ? The important question is, Am I surrendered to Christ *right now*? For the only life we have to surrender to Christ is the life we're living this moment.

Unfortunately, many Christians seem to have a "magical" understanding of Christianity that leads them to assume their life is surrendered to Christ because they once pledged to do just that. They pray a "sinner's prayer" and think that this somehow — magically — means they have a real relationship with Christ. But it doesn't, any more than making marriage vows magically produces a loving relationship between two people.

I believe this is the most prevalent and tragic misunderstanding that afflicts contemporary Western Christianity. We make a vow to submit our life to

Are you awake?

Christ but then spend 99 percent of our time excluding him from our awareness. We make him Lord over our life in *theory*, but we do not make him Lord over most of the moments that make up our life.

All that matters is . . . to belong totally to God, to please him, making our sole happiness to look on the present moment as though nothing else in the world mattered.

J.-P. de Caussade

For Jesus to be our Lord, he must be Lord over our actual life—the one we live moment-by-moment. The only relevant question is, Are we surrendering our life to Christ as Lord *right now*? Is this a moment in which we are aware of, and surrendered to, Christ's Lordship? Is this a moment over which God reigns as King? Are we, in this moment, living within the Kingdom of God?

The supersaints aren't the only ones who need to ask these questions. Living in this way is simply what it means to surrender our life—our *actual* life—to Christ.

The Heart of New Testament Discipleship

Once we set aside our compartmentalized, secular Western worldview, we discover that the New Testament tells us that disciples of Jesus are to remain aware of, and surrendered to, God's presence each moment. Here are some illustrations.

Seek First the Kingdom

Jesus tells us to "seek first the Kingdom of God" and

trust that God will provide us with all that we need (Matthew 6:33). But this isn't something we can do one moment and then forget the next. We can't pretend we're obeying Jesus and seeking God's Kingdom because we sought the Kingdom yesterday while today our sole focus is on a job promotion or a family matter or a new house. We can't imagine we're following Jesus' teachings to trust God to provide for us because we trusted him in the past while today we're obsessed with providing for ourselves.

No, to seek the Kingdom first means we need to seek the Kingdom in each of the present moments that comprise our actual life. It means that living under God's reign

> [Practicing the presence of God] is the secret of the great saints of all ages. "Pray without ceasing," said Paul, "in everything make your wants known unto God. As many as are led by the Spirit of God, these are the sons of God."
>
> Frank Laubach

is our highest aspiration right now. While we will, of course, have other goals on our mind in any given moment (such as understanding and internalizing the message of this book), the primary goal of each moment (including this one as you read this sentence) must be to make that moment one over which God reigns. This implies remembering that God exists and that yielding to his will is our supreme objective, even as we strive for other, less important, goals.

Living in the Spirit

The apostle Paul tells us that followers of Jesus are to

live in — and be led by — the Spirit (see Galatians 5:16–18, for example). Again, this isn't something we can do one moment and then forget the next. No, to live in the Spirit means that we submit to the Spirit in the present moment, for the only life we have to submit to the Spirit is the one we're living right now. To obey Paul's teaching, therefore, means that we learn to cultivate a surrendered awareness of the Holy Spirit moment-by-moment.

Remaining in Christ

Jesus teaches his followers to "remain" in him (John 15:4–5). The Greek word translated "remain," *menô*, means "to take up permanent residence." Jesus makes this clear when he says that just as branches are attached to a vine, we are to be attached to him (John 15:1–5). Branches don't visit a vine once in a while on special occasions. Rather, branches are permanently attached to their source of life. So too, followers of Jesus are to take up permanent residence in Christ, remaining attached to him at all times as their source of their Life.

> *I have found that we can establish ourselves in a sense of the presence of God by continually talking with Him.*
>
> Brother Lawrence

Praying Continually

Paul instructs us to pray continually (1 Thessalonians 5:17). While we do have to set aside time for concentrated dialogue with God, as Jesus did, the biblical model of prayer is that it should permeate our life. As Lawrence, de Caussade, and Laubach all teach, we should aspire to make our entire life a sustained conversation with God.

Take Every Thought Captive

Closely related to this, Paul says we are to take every thought captive to Christ and be transformed by the renewing of our mind (2 Corinthians 10:5; Romans 12:2).

I don't know if you've ever noticed it, but your brain never stops thinking. It's constantly chattering! If you doubt me, go into a quiet room, shut off the lights, and try not to think. Listen carefully for the voice in your head and see how long you can keep it completely silent. If you're attentive, you'll probably discover that within five to ten seconds

> The most wonderful discovery of all is, to use the words of Paul, "Christ liveth in me." He dwells in us, walks in our minds, reaches out through our hands, speaks with our voices, if we respond to His every whisper.
>
> Frank Laubach

you'll be chattering to yourself. You'll hear things like: "So far so good" or "This is stupid" or "Don't forget to take out the garbage."

Our brain never shuts up. To submit *every* thought to Christ, therefore, we're going to need to have Christ on our mind all the time.

This doesn't mean we should try to analyze every thought to make sure it's submitted to Christ. This would turn our mental focus completely onto ourselves and would pull us out of the present moment. It would also likely drive us crazy. Rather, to take every thought captive to Christ simply means to remain aware that he is ever-present and to surrender to him. Invite him into your thought process, and turn your thoughts into a conversation with him.

The Body of Christ

One final teaching worth noting is that disciples of Jesus belong to the corporate body of Christ (1 Corinthians 12:12 – 27; Romans 12:4 – 5). He is the head and we are his hands, feet, mouth, and so on (Ephesians 4:15; Colossians 1:18; 2:19). We all know what happens when a body part "falls asleep" — or worse, when its connection to the head gets severed. A foot that isn't connected to the head isn't going to be much of a foot. So too, before we can function as the body part we are called to be, we must stay continually connected to the head, ready to respond when he tells us to do so.

> One may never get to the point where they continually are in God's presence. You may not win all your minutes to Christ, or even half, but you do win a richer life. There are no losers excepting those who quit.
>
> Frank Laubach

These are just a few of the teachings of the New Testament that presuppose that the "normal" life of a disciple is to remain aware of God's presence. As foreign as it is to contemporary Western Christianity, and as impossible as it may seem to many contemporary Christians, practicing the presence of God lies at the foundation of "mere Christianity."

To passionately embrace this call as the central goal of your life, it is important to refrain from thinking about the magnitude of this challenge over an entire lifetime. Don't even worry about whether you'll be up to meeting this challenge tomorrow or a minute from now. The only thing that is real — and thus the only thing that is important — is right now. This challenge can only be met one moment at a time.

Right now is the time to surrender. Right now is the time to seek first the Kingdom of God. Right now is the time to remain in Christ, to live in the Spirit, to pray, and to take every thought captive. As Jesus taught, tomorrow will worry about itself (Matthew 6:34).

EXERCISES

Game with Minutes

Frank Laubach created something he called the "Game with Minutes" as a way to become more consistent in practicing God's presence. This game challenges us to bring Christ to mind at least one second of each and every minute within a designated hour. He called it a "game" both because he wanted it to be "lighthearted" and because he found it to be "a delightful experience and an exhilarating spiritual exercise."

Laubach recommends that we begin by designating a particular "uncomplicated hour" to "see how many minutes of the hour you can remember ... Christ at least once each minute." The basic idea is that we need to become accustomed to remembering Christ when our mind has little to do before we can learn how to remember Christ with any consistency in situations that require more attention.

To begin this "game," think about the times when you tend to be most bored. Designate one or more of these periods as a time in which you're going to challenge yourself to remember Christ at least once every minute. I find I play the "game" most effectively when I'm jogging, mowing the lawn, washing the dishes, or engaging in some other mindless task. Not only does this practice transform a boring activity into a sacred moment, it makes the boring activity much more interesting and helps the time pass more quickly. Staying awake to God's presence helps you experience the wonder of shear existence, regardless of how boring the activity you're engaged in is.

Waking Up to God

For many of us, the most "uncomplicated" time of any day is when we first wake up. Our heart and mind are clearest before they get filled with the cares and concerns of the day. Not surprisingly, biblical authors as well as spiritual leaders throughout history have expressed a preference for worshiping, praying, and meditating on God as the first act of every day (for instance, Psalm 5:3; 59:16; 88:13; 90:14). Laubach himself testified that he found it helpful to practice the presence when he first woke up in the morning, especially when he first embarked on this discipline. Each morning, he said, "I compel my mind to open straight out toward God." He then added, "I wait and listen with determined sensitiveness. I fix my attention there, and sometimes it requires a long time early in the morning. I determine not to get out of bed until that mind set upon the Lord is settled."

I too have found the practice of surrendering the first moments of waking consciousness to God to be profoundly helpful. At first it was hard to remember to practice the presence before getting out of bed, but I now find that, more often than not, God is automatically the first thought on my mind. For ten or fifteen minutes I lie in bed and simply try to remain aware of God's ever-present love. After this, I preview my day in my imagination and offer up everything to God. I typically follow this by praying for whatever people and needs that pop into my mind.

As a general rule, I find practicing God's presence first thing in the morning affects my awareness throughout the rest of the day. I also find that I tend to *experience* God's presence most profoundly in the morning, probably because my mind has not yet become cluttered with the busyness of life. I suspect many readers will find the same is true for them if they are diligent in committing the very first segment of each day to God.

Inviting Fellow Travelers

As we embark on the discipline of practicing the presence of God, we need to remember that we are seeking to do nothing less than expand and transform our consciousness. All our life we've practiced *forgetting* God; now we're seeking to *remember* him. This is as formidable a challenge as we could ever undertake, and we will need all the help we can get.

For this reason, Frank Laubach encourages us to invite others to join us. "We need the stimulus of believers who pursue what we pursue, the presence of God," he writes. Thus, I encourage you to ask a friend, or a group of friends, to embark on this discipline with you. Give each other permission to randomly ask one another throughout the day, "Are you awake?" Encourage one another as you face obstacles or go through "bad patches" — periods of time after which you realize you've forgotten God is always with you. Help each other by sharing tips you've found helpful in staying awake.

Strategically Placed Reminders

It helps to embed little reminders in your environment that will bring you back to an awareness of God in the present moment. Try posting sticky notes in places that you'll see throughout the day. (You'll want to change these frequently so they don't just become "wallpaper.") Try associating the practice of God's presence with a piece of jewelry that you wear or a stone or cross that you carry in your pocket. A friend of mine wears a rubber band around his wrist to help him to remember to stay awake. If you work at a computer, set up an automatic reminder in your calendar each hour or half hour. Think about your environment and your routine and imagine all of the ways you could slip little reminders into the nooks and crannies of your life. Before you know it, you'll be finding your mind turning toward Jesus more and more.

Chapter 2

Finding Home

I am trying to be utterly free from everybody,
free from my own self,
but completely enslaved to the will of God
every moment of this day.

Frank Laubach

Our ever-present Creator,
you alone can satisfy the hunger in our hearts,
for you made us for yourself.
Help us to relinquish all idols
and to find our fulfillment
solely in you
in this moment
and in every moment.

Our Insatiable Hunger

The only kind of life animals care about is biological. If their basic physical needs for food and shelter are met, they're satisfied. Humans also want their basic physical needs met, of course, but that isn't enough. We hunger for more. Not only do we want to be alive, we want to feel *fully* alive. We hunger for Life.

This craving for Life can be described in many ways. Among other things, it includes the profound desire to feel loved and the desire to be happy. But one of the most fundamental aspects of the Life we long for is our undeniable, universal need to experience worth and significance. Though we may be unaware of it, all of us are driven by a desperate need to feel like we matter. Even if all our basic physical needs are met and we enjoy all the comforts the world has to offer, still, on some level, we will feel empty, unless we sense that our life serves an ultimate purpose.

Love so insatiable as the love of God can never be satisfied until we respond to the limit.

Frank Laubach

Many things can make us feel worthwhile and significant, but our deepest hunger is only satisfied when we're rightly related to God. Only our Creator can give us the fullness of Life we crave. Jesus' death on the cross is proof that we could not possibly have more worth and significance to God. Despite our sin, our Creator thinks we are worth experiencing a hellish death for. In fact, it was for the joy of spending eternity with us that Jesus endured the cross (Hebrews 12:2). In other words, Calvary reveals our unsurpassable worth and significance. At the core of our being, *this* is what we long for.

Why did God create us with this hunger? Because he wants to share himself with us. He wants us to participate in his divine nature (1 Peter 1:4). As Father, Son, and Holy Spirit, he longs for us to join in his eternal dance of perfect, ecstatic love. Our insatiable hunger for a depth

All he wishes is to be the sole object and only enchantment of our hearts.

J.-P. de Caussade

of Life that only he can give is a sort of built-in "homing device" intended to lead us to him. The Trinity is our home, and we are never fully satisfied or at peace until we rest in him.

Yet because God wants a loving relationship with us, he does not force us to accept his invitation. We have the ability to refuse it if we so choose. If we want, we can pretend we're self-sufficient and able to meet our own needs. In fact, were it not for God's grace working in our life, this is what all of us in our fallen condition would want and what all of us would choose. For apart from Christ, Scripture says, we are all dead in our sins (Ephesians 2:1, 5).

When we push God away, our homing device doesn't shut off. It simply gets redirected. Instead of leading us home to the Trinity, we try to satisfy our hunger for worth and significance by turning to other things.

False Gods

We often think of an idol as a statue, but an idol can be anything we use to meet the need that only God can meet. In other words, a false god.

There is no end to the false gods we create when our homing device gets misdirected. In Western cultures we often strive to feel worth and significance by acquiring money, possessions, and power. We bow down to the false gods of materialism and control. Some try to relieve their inner emptiness by trying to get approval for being sexy, talented, or successful.

If a Christian is to truly practice the presence of his Lord ... then the heart of that Christian must be empty of all else. All. Why? Because God wills ... to be the only possessor of that heart.

Brother Lawrence

They bow down to a false god of fame. Some feed their hunger for Life by convincing themselves they're special to God because they believe all the right things and engage in all the right behaviors — in contrast to others who believe the wrong things and engage in all the wrong behaviors. These bow before the false god of religion. And still others try to assuage their pervasive sense of emptiness by feeling superior on the basis of their family name, ethnic heritage, or national identity. These bow before the false god of tribalism.

The list goes on, but the point is clear. *Whatever* we try to derive our core sense of worth and meaning from is our god.[1]

Beliefs and Reality

Of course, when we chase after false gods, we seldom realize what we're doing. We don't think of it as idolatry. In fact, it's possible to bow to false gods while believing you're bowing to Jesus Christ. For what we believe often has little to do with reality.

I've observed that we in the West—especially Christians—tend to attach great importance to what we believe. We treat beliefs almost as though they have magical power, as though merely believing something makes it so. For instance, many assume that *believing* Jesus is Lord of their life magically *makes* him Lord. This is undoubtedly why so many evangelical churches place so much significance on getting people to believe in Jesus and why so much is made of the moment sinners raise their hand or go to the altar to profess their faith in Jesus. This one-time

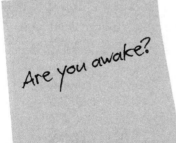

Are you awake?

event, it is often assumed, makes Jesus Lord of their life forever.

The truth is, merely believing Jesus is Lord no more makes him Lord of my life than believing Kim Jong-il is the leader of North Korea makes me his follower. For Kim Jong-il to be my leader, I would need to submit my life to him and become a citizen of North Korea. So too, for Jesus to be my Lord, I need to submit my life to him and become a citizen of his Kingdom.

Research shows that however emotional people may have been when they raised their hand or responded to the altar call, fewer than 4 percent reflected any change in their lives several years later.

I'm not trying to minimize the importance of beliefs. Obviously, it's impossible to surrender to Jesus unless you first believe that he is Lord. Still, the belief is not itself the surrender. Embracing a belief is something you do in your mind. Actually surrendering your life is something you can only do with your will. And since the only life you have to surrender is the one you're living in this present moment, the decision to surrender can only take place right now.

We should seek our satisfaction only in satisfying his will.

Brother Lawrence

The important question, therefore, is not *what* you believe. The important question is what you decide to do, moment-by-moment, on the basis of what you believe.

The Futility of Idols

While our culture conditions us to place great hope in our idols, the truth is that they never permanently satisfy us. However successful we might be by the world's standards —through money, wealth, power, fame—we always hunger for more. Regardless of how much we get, sooner or later we want more.

Most of us try to sustain the illusion that we're self-sufficient by denying our emptiness. But the symptoms are undeniable. For some, this inner emptiness is manifested in anxiety or anger. For others it's a gnawing sense of alienation, depression, or frustration. Still others experience it as relentless boredom or apathy toward life.

Some try to distract themselves from this hole-in-the-soul by obsessing about work, sports, politics, or a hobby. Others numb themselves to their inner pain with alcohol, drugs, or sexual addiction. But whatever relief such strategies offer, it's temporary. Sooner or later the painful hunger returns.

As long as we refuse God's invitation and continue to buy the lie that Life can be found outside of a relationship with God, we

> *Money, praise, poverty, opposition, these make no difference, for they will all alike be forgotten in a thousand years, but this spirit which comes to a mind set upon continuous surrender, this spirit is timeless life.*
>
> Frank Laubach

continue to think our problem is that we simply don't have enough. If only we had more of our idol, we imagine, or perhaps if only we tried a different idol, *then* we'd feel alive. It's all a grand illusion.

Living "As Though"

The Bible refers to this grand illusion as life in "the flesh" (*sarx*), and it's the main obstacle that keeps us from finding true Life.[2] Our minds are blinded by "the god of this age" (2 Corinthians 4:4) so that we keep living *as though* what is true is false and what is false is true.

When we live *as though* we were lords of our own life, capable of meeting our own needs, we are living in the flesh. When we treat people, possessions, or achievements *as though* they were the source of our worth and significance rather than God, we are living in the flesh. In fact, insofar as we live *as though* God were not present, moment-by-moment, and *as though* this wasn't the most important aspect of any present moment, we are living in the flesh.

Living *as though* God was not our only true source of Life forces us to live most of our life in the past and future — *as though* the present moment was not the only reality. While the true God lives in the now, false gods always live in the past or future. Chasing them to find our worth and significance always takes us out of the present moment.

If you doubt this, investigate your own soul. How much of your thought-life is spent in the past or future, and what is the purpose for this nonpresent thinking? You may be so accustomed to living in the past and future that you find it difficult to notice how much of your thought-life is spent there, let alone *why* you spend so much of your thought-life there. But if you are completely honest with yourself, you'll probably find that most of your past and future orientated thoughts revolve around *you* and are centered on your attempts to feel worthwhile and significant.

When we live perpetually hungry in the flesh, we spend a great deal of our thought-life savoring past experiences or possible future experiences that make us feel more worthwhile and significant. We also spend a great deal of time ruminating over past experiences or worrying about possible future experiences that will make us feel less worthwhile and significant. All the while we are strategizing over how to position ourselves to have more of the worth-giving experiences and how to better avoid the worth-detracting experiences.

Discard idols, and the senses will cry like disappointed children, but faith triumphs for it can never be estranged from God's will.

J.-P. de Caussade

Most of us are so accustomed to being hungry for Life and living in the past and future that we don't realize this is what we're doing. It's hard for a fish to notice the water it swims in. But the fact of the matter is that we are rarely in the present moment when we're hungry and chasing after false gods. This is yet another aspect of the grand illusion that entraps us. The very process of trying to acquire Life on our own forces us to miss most of life, for real life is always in the present moment. When we live *as though* we can acquire Life from things other than God, we inevitably live *as though* reality wasn't always in the present moment.

Only a person who is no longer driven by an insatiable hunger can consistently live in the present moment, and only a person who has learned how to find Life in the present moment is no longer driven by this insatiable hunger.

Reorienting the Homing Device

The only way we can experience the fullness of Life is to give up trying to acquire it on our own. We must surrender ourselves completely to God. This is not merely a matter of believing that our attempts to acquire worth and significance are idolatrous and unsatisfying. A person can easily believe this and yet fail to relinquish their idols and surrender to God. We enter into the Life of God only when our false gods have in fact been relinquished and only when God is in fact reigning over our life.

I can lie down anywhere in this universe bathed around by my own Father's Spirit. The very universe has come to seem so homey!

Frank Laubach

To the extent that our sense of worth and significance is caught up in the grand illusion — to the extent that our

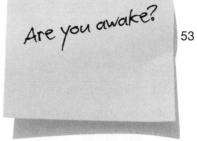
Are you awake?

identity is rooted in the "flesh" — abandoning our false gods will feel like a kind of death. In fact, it *is* a kind of death, for the "old self" that relied on idols to feel worthwhile and significant is being killed. This is why Jesus says we must lose our life in order to find real Life and why Paul testified he was crucified with Christ (Matthew 16:25; Galatians 2:20; 5:24; 6:14).

Still, as scary and as difficult as dying to the false way of living may initially be, nothing could be more liberating. Living with perpetual hunger, spending most of our mental life in the past and future, chasing after pathetic false gods, is complete bondage. When we cling to things that are perpetually threatened and that we know we'll eventually lose, it inevitably creates in us worry, anger, jealousy, envy, frustration, strife, violence, and despair — things Paul referred to as "works of the flesh" (Galatians 5:19 KJV). To die to the flesh is the greatest liberation possible. Now one is in a position to live in the moment and feel fully alive.

As we are freed from the grand illusion that we can meet our own needs, our built-in homing device begins to work correctly. We're on our way home. And we don't have to strive to find it. On the contrary, the instant we relinquish the world of idols and turn to God, he is there. He has always been there. In him we live and move and have our being (Acts 17:28). He never leaves us or forsakes us, whether we are aware of him or not (Matthew 28:20). There is nowhere we can run and hide from his presence (Psalm 139:8).

The moment we surrender, we are home. In fact, the moment we stop chasing and clinging we discover that we never really left home. Like Dorothy in *The Wizard of Oz*, we wake up from a dream and discover that all we've been looking for surrounds us at every moment. When we stop looking at the world *as though* God didn't exist, we find we are surrounded each and every moment with a love that infuses our life with a worth and significance that couldn't possibly be improved on. *This* is the home we were created to eternally live in.

Coming home is simply a matter of waking up from the illusion that you aren't already there. Yet, while the *belief* that the love of God is our home can be embraced at one moment and then forgotten about, the *actual decision* to release the illusion and embrace the truth cannot. As with everything else that pertains to our actual life, this act can only be done one moment at a time.

The only thing that matters is that we — right now — cease our striving after false gods and become aware of God's ever-present, perfect love.

EXERCISES

Finding "Home" in Your Skin

For much of my life I've felt a little bit like an alien. I'm sure many of you know exactly what I'm talking about. To be completely honest, there are still times when I just don't feel completely "at home" in my own skin or in any environment. For most of his life Frank Laubach felt the same way. In fact, he struggled with a profound sense of loneliness, anxiety, and depression.

At the age of forty-five, however, he discovered that practicing the presence of God eradicated these feelings. He became continually aware that wherever he went and whatever circumstances he found himself in, he was "bathed around by my own Father's Spirit" so the whole universe came "to seem so homey." As a result, Laubach found that worry, anxiety, alienation, fear, and loneliness pretty much left him.

I haven't had the complete breakthrough Laubach seems to have had, but I have found that my sense of alienation has largely dissipated as a result of practicing the presence. I feel much more "at home" in my skin — and in the universe — than I used to. Here's an exercise that has helped me experience God's closeness and helped me feel "at home," regardless of my circumstances. It involves using the incredible gift of your physical body to help you remember God's ever-present love and care for you.

Think for a moment about the way God designed the world and the laws of nature to support you. Unless you're living in a zero-gravity environment, your body is always in contact with something and is always being supported in multiple ways. For example, at this moment your feet are probably being supported by the floor and your body is probably resting on a chair or sofa. When you lie down tonight, your body will be supported by your bed. Your skin is always touching some other part of the physical world, and that touch can be transformed into a little signal from the Father that he is watching over you and caring for you.

In this moment, turn your attention to the points of contact between your body and the things that are supporting your weight. Become aware of the weight of your body against the chair, your feet against the floor, and so on.... Allow yourself to rest in that support and realize that every point of contact reflects the truth that you are held in existence each and every moment by the perfect love of God (Hebrews 1:3). God is personally holding you securely in the world. He cares that you have places to rest. Throughout your day, turn your attention over and over again to these physical points of contact and transform those physical sensations into a deeper awareness of the great love of God.

Engaging in this discipline, I have found that I feel much more at home in the world because my continual contact with the world has become a sacrament communicating to me I'm always at home in God's loving presence.

Experiencing God's Fullness of Life

All three of the authors we're reflecting on in this book stress the need for people to find all their satisfaction, fulfillment, and happiness — what I'm calling Life — in God alone. Everything involved in the Christian life is to be done not as a way of *getting* Life but as a means of *expressing* the Life we already have from Christ for free. Experiencing fullness of Life, therefore, is the foundation for everything. Here are two exercises that help me open up to experiencing God's fullness of Life.

1. As I become mindful of how God cares for me by supporting me in the world, I whisper truths to myself such as:

> "I could not possibly be more loved than I am this moment."
>
> "This instant I have unsurpassable worth and infinite significance because of Calvary."
>
> "All I *really* need I already have in Christ, right here and right now."
>
> "In this moment I am submerged in an infinite ocean of God's love and delight over me."
>
> "My life is Christ, nothing else really matters."

Since our mind thinks with images, I intentionally imagine God's loving presence around me like an ocean, a warm glowing bubble, or a mist as I recite these truths. I also sometimes imagine myself so full of God's love that it exudes from me like light from a very bright lightbulb. The Holy Spirit may give you different ways of mentally representing God's presence all around you.

As you engage in this discipline, it's important to realize that these are not psychological tricks to make us feel better about ourselves. God *is* present and we *are* filled

with his Life, so in thinking this way we are simply getting our minds to line up with reality. It's also helpful to
know that, generally speaking, the more concrete we can
represent truths in our mind via our imagination, the more
power they have to impact us.[3] So ask the Spirit to give you
a vivid way of representing God's ever-present love and Life
in your mind. Watch how reciting and representing these
truths helps anchor you in the present moment and opens
you up to experiencing God's eternally full Life.

2. A second discipline that I find indispensable is this:
I set aside regular times when I darken a room, play some
nice background music, and imaginatively see, hear, and
sense Jesus pouring his perfect love on me. As vividly as
possible, I see, hear, and sense Jesus expressing to me all
the things Scripture says about me, but now these truths
are intimate, personal, and, therefore, much more impacting. This is called "cataphatic [or imaginative] prayer" in
the church tradition and multitudes have found it to be a
powerful way of experiencing and being transformed by the
fullness of Life that come from Christ alone.[4]

Chapter 3

Chasing the Sun

I am in a calm so great
that I fear nothing.
What could I fear?
I am with Him.

Brother Lawrence

Eternal, ever-present Creator,
help us to see
your love as the background
against which we view all things.
Free us to let go of the world
that is fading away
and to cling only to you.
Keep us awake to your presence
in this moment
and in every moment.

Are you awake?

Wasting Away

In my humble (but indisputably correct) opinion, one of the greatest rock songs of all time is Pink Floyd's "Time," recorded on what is incontestably the single greatest rock album of all time, *Dark Side of the Moon*. Carefully read the following lyrics (though, if it's at all possible, I encourage you to take a break and listen to the actual song).

Ticking away the moments that make up a dull day
Fritter and waste the hours in an offhand way
Kicking around on a piece of ground in your home town;
Waiting for someone or something to show you the way

Tired of lying in the sunshine staying home to watch the rain
You are young and life is long and there is time to kill today
And then one day you find ten years have got behind you
No one told you when to run, you missed the starting gun

*And you run and you run to catch up with the sun, but
    it's sinking
Racing around to come up behind you again
The sun is the same in the relative way, but you're older
Shorter of breath and one day closer to death*

*Every year is getting shorter, never seem to find the time
Plans that either come to naught or half a page of scrib-
    bled lines
Hanging on in quiet desperation is the English way
The time is gone, the song is over,
thought I'd something more to say . . .*

Powerful lyrics.

I'm writing this just before my fifty-third birthday. I find it almost impossible to believe I'm that old; a part of me still thinks (and acts) like a teenager. I have two daughters who are both married and have children. Wasn't I changing their diapers yesterday? Surely it wasn't twenty-two years ago I caught them sneaking around at five o'clock on Christmas morning to see what Santa had brought them? It seems like yesterday.

We have only to welcome divine eternity in the passing shadows of time.

J.-P. de Caussade

When you're young, life seems long and you think there's time to kill. But one day you wonder where the last ten years have gone. Then the next ten years go by even faster. So we run and we run to catch up to the sun, but it's sinking, racing around to come up behind us again. The reappearing sun is always the same, relatively speaking, but we aren't. We're shorter of breath and one day closer to death.

I often feel as if I'm on a train that's constantly picking up speed as it races toward a brick wall. I have no idea when I'll crash, but I know I won't survive. Each passing moment takes me closer to this inevitability at an ever-increasing speed.

I'm dying. We're all dying. Some of us are at an age where we can actually *feel* it. In the introduction I mentioned that I used to race in 100-kilometer ultramarathons. Now my back aches and I feel out of breath after jogging three miles. I don't know when this began, but last year I noticed that I often grunt whenever I get up from a chair or bend over.

I always used to understand where my pains came from. Now aches and pains just pop up for no apparent reason. Two months ago my elbow began aching. Last week I began to feel an occasional numbness in three fingers. I'll have a doctor check it when I have time. But whatever he finds, it's ultimately just typical body decay.

> I have no pain and no doubt in my present state, because I have no will but God's.
>
> Brother Lawrence

I'm dying. We're all dying.

In fact, every passing moment is a kind of death. The moment is here, utterly unique and unrepeatable, and then it's gone forever. Every moment is filled with possibilities, most of which we have to pass by, and most of which are gone for good once we pass them by. We die each and every moment.

Once you could have been a model, a rock star, a professional athlete, a great scholar, a missionary — whatever your dream happened to be. Now, depending on your age and situation, that possibility may be closed. Perhaps you simply chose a different path. Perhaps something prevented your dream from happening. Or maybe you just never got around to making it happen.

This present, if it is full of God, is the only refuge I have from poisonous disappointment and even almost rebellion against God.

Frank Laubach

Your plans just came to naught or remained half a page of scribbled lines. And now, you realize, it's too late.

You can go ahead and run to catch up with the sun if you'd like, but, along with Pink Floyd, I assure you it's going to sink before you catch it, only to mock you by coming up behind you again. It'll be pretty much the same; but you'll be shorter of breath and one day closer to death.

This perpetual, relentless process of decay, leading inevitably toward death, fills many of us with a certain amount of angst. Some try to relieve their dread by immersing themselves in mind-numbing entertainment or chemical substances. Others try to live vicariously through their kids or through celebrities. Some become addicted to new thrills, new sexual escapades, new bouts of falling in love, or anything else that can temporarily stave off the sense of getting older by creating the illusion of newness. And some simply try not to think about it by pouring themselves into their work or some other interest.

In the youth-worshiping culture of the West, some who can afford it fight the relentless march of time with Botox, face lifts, tummy tucks, breast enhancements, and an assortment of other anti-aging techniques. Others try to desperately hold on to their "glory days," as Bruce Springsteen sang, by dreaming about their wonderful past. Reaching middle age and disappointed with their life, some try to actually go back and relive their "glory days." It's called a "midlife crisis" and often causes tremendous pain for family and friends. Of course, some people, like the English whom Pink Floyd sang about, simply "hang on in quiet desperation," covering their dread and despair with a polite but forced smile.

Are you awake?

The fear is not just that we're going to die. The fear is that we'll never really live. We fear coming to the point at which the "song is over" and we realize we don't have as much to say as we thought we would.

Once we had dreams. We were going to be somebody. Our life, our achievements, our impact, our marriage, our family was going to be exceptional. But for most of us, the unrelenting monotonous cycle of days has dampened, and perhaps even snuffed out, many of these dreams.

It turns out we are not exceptional. Along with most people, we live and die in mediocrity.

The Curse and Liberation

This isn't how things were supposed to be. The decay, death, and futility we experience in our life and witness throughout creation is not part of the Creator's original design. Rather, it's the result of a curse we brought upon ourselves. Humans were supposed to be God's caring viceroys on earth, but instead we surrendered our authority to Satan and other fallen powers. All decay, sickness, death, and destruction is ultimately the result of the influence of these rebel spirits.[1]

Troubles and pains come to those who practice God's presence, as they came to Jesus, but these seem not so important as compared to their new joyous experience ... "Perfect love casteth out fear."

Frank Laubach

The good news is that God has not abandoned us in this cursed environment. He has promised us that the creation will eventually be restored to his original ideal. In fact, though we don't see it yet, in Christ God has already, in principle, defeated the principalities and powers and brought about a "new creation"

(2 Corinthians 5:17). It's just a matter of time before all decay, death, and futility are abolished forever.

Fear, Dread, and the Passage of Time

In the meantime, however, we suffer. Until God establishes his kingdom on the earth, we can't escape decay and death. But we can, right now, escape the fear and dread that many experience as a result of this. For right now, in the midst of our perpetually decaying environment, God is present. While we are physically dying every moment, the One who is eternal Life invites us to participate in his Life each moment. While everything around us crumbles to the ground, the One who never came into being and who cannot pass away invites us, each moment, to share in the eternal sameness and perfect security of his perfect love. While the reign of God will only be fully established in the future, we can make each moment of our life a moment over which God reigns, simply by submitting to him.

What is the secret of how to find this treasure [of God's presence] — this minute grain of mustard seed? There is none. It is available to us always, everywhere.

J.-P. de Caussade

Because death and decay are unnatural, it's to be expected that we experience them as unpleasant and that we grieve when loved ones pass away. But the fear and dread people experience in response to their decay and the passing away of the world is something completely different.

For this is nothing more than a by-product of living "in the flesh."

Regardless of what we may believe in theory, we experience fear and dread over the decay of our body and our impending death only because we are in fact viewing our present preciously short life as though it were our total life. We feel angst to the extent that we

While I am with Him I fear nothing.

Brother Lawrence

live as though our worth and significance was wrapped up with the vitality of our body and intellect and all that we might accomplish with our body and intellect. We experience fear and dread to the extent that we live as though true Life could be found by being exceptional and fulfilling all the dreams of our youth.

We need to wake up to the truth that this is all part of the grand illusion of the flesh.

Our physical and intellectual vitality — as well as the hope of being exceptional and fulfilling the dreams of our youth — become false gods when our core worth and significance are wrapped up in them. Chasing and striving after these things takes us out of the present moment, anchoring us instead in the past and future.

To the extent that we live in the flesh and thus operate out of a center of hunger, we can't help but long for the more vigorous mind and body of our youth. Nor can we help being anxious over the further decay and ultimate death of our mind and body in the future.

To the extent that we are defined by this false way of living, we can't help but lament past dreams that were not fulfilled and be anxious over the demise of those few dreams we managed to fulfill. Nor can we help feeling empty over how average our lives turned out or worrying that when the song is over we won't have something more to say.

Stop now and agree with the Lord to live the rest of your days in His sacred presence. Then, out of love for Him, surrender all other pleasures.

Brother Lawrence

To the extent that we are living as though the present wasn't the only reality and as though God's presence wasn't the all-important aspect of present reality, we can't help but suffer fear and dread as we see the futility of clinging to things that are being ripped from our grasp, moment-by-moment.

To the extent that our worth and significance are wrapped up in things that come into being and that pass away, we cannot help but be obsessed with the past and future and cannot avoid the fear and dread that this obsession produces.

Freedom from Fear and Dread

Freedom from fear and dread is one decision away, and it can be made in this moment. In fact, it can *only* be made in this moment. Freedom is simply a matter of letting go of everything as a source of ultimate worth and significance as we surrender ourselves completely to our ever-present, loving Father.

Why wait? If you have any element of anxiety in your life, do this exercise. (I encourage you to do this even if you *aren't* aware of any anxiety in your life.)

Begin by reminding yourself that the only thing that is real is this moment, and the only thing that ultimately matters is that you are submerged in God's love right now. Remain mindful of the fact that the perfect love that God expressed by becoming a human and dying on a cross to redeem you engulfs you, right now. Remind yourself that you could not be more loved than you are this moment. You could not have more worth than you have this moment. Your life could not be more significant than it is at this moment. Remain mindful of the truth that this is not because of anything you have achieved or ever will achieve in your life.

It's because of who God is and who you are, as defined by Calvary. Remind yourself that this perfect love never began, never ends, is never threatened, and never wavers. As you breathe your next breath, let it represent your decision to breathe in God's loving presence and all these truths associated with it.

I came to the realization that I should put aside all the thoughts which brought about these times of trouble and unrest. Immediately I found myself changed. My soul, which had been so troubled, then felt a profound sense of inward peace and rest.

Brother Lawrence

As you breathe in God's love, exhale everything else. Because God loves you, trust that if there's anything you truly need God will give it to you, as Jesus taught us (Matthew 6:32–33). Relinquish (exhale) all your possessions, achievements, reputation, future aspirations, health, beauty, relationships, and anything else that could possibly be a false source of worth and significance to you. As you relax in the sufficiency of God's presence, see all these potential idols evaporate in the light of God's ever-present love, like a morning mist disappearing with the first rays of the rising sun.

Now, while continuing to remain aware of God's presence, notice what happened to whatever anxiety you may have had. If you are truly present, breathing in God's love and exhaling everything else, you will have found that your anxiety has disappeared.

This concentration upon God is so strenuous, but everything else has ceased to be so. I think more clearly, I forget less frequently. Things which I did with a strain before, I now do easily and with no effort whatever. I worry about nothing, and lose no sleep.

Frank Laubach

If you are truly present, it cannot help but disappear — just as it cannot help but reappear if you once again begin to cling to idols and get pulled out of the present moment. For as we've seen, our fear and dread are directly associated with our pursuit of idols and, therefore, being pulled out of the present into the past or future. To relinquish the idols and remain in the present, surrender to God's ever-present love.

In this way the practice of the presence of God completely frees us from the fear of death. Freedom from anxiety is one of the surest evidences you are learning how to abide in Christ moment-by-moment. If we remain surrendered to God, we've already died to everything decay and death could ever threaten to take away. Our treasure is no longer in things that moths can eat and thieves can steal (Matthew 6:19 – 20). Our heart is no longer set on things that aging and misfortune can affect. Our life is securely hidden in Christ, whose love never changes (Colossians 3:1 – 3). In fact, to the extent that we're surrendered to God every moment, we've "been crucified with Christ and [we] no longer live, but Christ lives in [us]" (Galatians 2:20).

This is why Jesus told his disciples never to worry — despite the fact that they were going to face persecution and death (Matthew 6:25 – 34). When God's love becomes our sole source of Life moment-by-moment, we will have no regrets about the past and no fears about the future, for we are fulfilled and are trusting God in the present. We learn from our past mistakes, of course, and make ordinary plans about the future.

Students can keep Christ in mind even when taking an exam by saying things like, "Father, keep my mind clear.... How shall we answer this next questions?" He will not tell you what you have never studied, but He does sharpen your memory and take away your stage fright when you ask Him.

Frank Laubach

But anchored in the fullness of God's abundant Life right now, we're freed from the pointless, idolatrous exercise of judging our past or stressing out over the future.

The only thing that matters is now, and it is filled with God's loving presence.

Does Practicing the Presence Lead to Inactivity?

Some may fear that if they rest in God's love they will lose their drive to be the best they can be in school, in their careers, or even in their ministry. As one concerned parent objected after hearing me speak on this topic to a youth group, "My son needs drive if he's ever going to amount to anything in this world."

This fear arises from people who are only familiar with what we might call *hunger-motivation*. If we are living in "the flesh," the thing that drives us is hunger. Though few are aware of it, we try to feel significant by achieving, acquiring, or accomplishing things. A person who has learned how to get their Life from God each moment loses this motivation. Consequently, they may not achieve, acquire, or accomplish as much as hungry, driven people do. They may not be as successful by the world's standards.

But the more we train our minds to remember God moment-by-moment, the more we discover an entirely different kind of motivation for doing things. We no longer engage in activities in a desperate and futile attempt to acquire Life we don't yet have; rather, we engage in them as a means of

Are you awake?

expressing the fullness of Life we already have—apart from these activities. The irony is that when a person no longer needs to succeed to feel fully worthwhile and significant they will tend to be more successful than if they did need this. When we need to achieve, acquire, and accomplish things to find Life, the pressure often compromises our passion, creativity, and flexibility.

A clear example of this was a student I had in one of my introductory theology classes at Bethel University a number of years ago. She was clearly brilliant, as evidenced by her class participation, but she was

O boundless submission.... Let the senses feel what they may, you, Lord, are all my good.... I have nothing more to see or do, not a single moment of my life is in my own hands. All is yours, I have nothing to add, remove, seek or consider.

J.-P. de Caussade

performing poorly on her tests. When I looked into the problem, I discovered that this young woman was putting incredible pressure on herself to succeed. Among other things, she believed her parents' approval hung on her getting straight A's and graduating as the valedictorian of her class, just as her two older siblings had done. If ever there was a class she feared not getting an A in, it was in theology, a topic she said she'd always had trouble relating to.

After some counseling I was able to help her realize that her core worth didn't depend on how she performed in school or on what her parents thought about her. Her real worth was rooted solely in what God thought about her, and this was unconditionally expressed on Calvary. I encouraged her to remain aware that she was surrounded by this love throughout the day and especially when she took her theology tests. She immediately began getting near perfect scores in my class—precisely because she no longer needed to.

The bottom line is that we were meant to live life as a celebration of a fullness of Life we get from God rather than as a desperate attempt to get fullness of Life on our own. People whose identity is solidly rooted in God's love moment-by-moment still try to do their best. But they do so because only this expresses their unsurpassable worth and significance. Moreover, they are now doing all that they do for the Lord who of course deserves our best.

If disciples who practice the presence of God fail to acquire the wealth, fame, and power that others do, it's because these things hold no interest for them any longer, not because they aren't motivated to do their best in whatever God calls them to engage in.

Living Out of the Center

Surrendered to God's presence in each present moment, we fulfill our "duty to the present moment" as best we can, for we are people who celebrate the fullness of Life we have from God and who do all we do as an act of worship to God. And we are empowered to do this because we have been freed from chasing after false gods and freed from obsessing on the past and future. We don't regret the past or fear the future, for we've lost nothing and can gain nothing that affects our unsurpassable worth and significance. We know that we are, in this moment, engulfed in a perfect love that never began and never ends, and all we do flows out of this center of peace and satisfaction.

Living in the present moment, we no longer need to chase the sinking sun. We no longer need to chase anything. All that we need we already have, right here, right now.

The only relevant question is, Can we remember this truth in this moment, or will our idol chasing, nonpresent, habitual thoughts take over? We can't answer this question for any future moments. Nor need we condemn or applaud ourselves for how we answered it in past moments. We can only answer this question in this present moment.

And now in this one.

EXERCISES

Letting Go

As we've seen, Lawrence, de Caussade, and Laubach all stress our need to completely let go of the world as a source of Life if we're going to offer ourselves up to God moment-by-moment. "All things hinge upon your hearty renunciation of everything which you are aware does not lead to God," Brother Lawrence says. To the extent that we cling to false sources of Life, our mind invariably gravitates toward the past or future as it develops idolatrous, self-serving strategies to get Life. We thus fail to surrender to our true source of Life moment-by-moment.

Now, these three authors also stress that it won't do you any good to turn the call to relinquish idols into a contest with yourself. This will become just another idol from which you futilely try to derive Life! Getting mad at the things you're overly attached to—or mad at yourself for being overly attached to them—is never helpful.

To get free of our idol addiction and become aware of God's presence one has to simply "let go," as Laubach put it. "The reason I didn't have it [a sense of God's 'hereness'] before was because I failed to let go," he says. And like everything else about life, this decision to "let go" can't be made in one moment and then set aside. It can only be done in each present moment.

In this chapter we alluded to an exercise that I and many others have found helpful in learning how to continually "let go." It is rooted in the fact that we are embodied beings. This means that the physical and spiritual dimensions of our being—our body and soul—are intimately wrapped up with one another. As we found with the "find home in your skin" exercise in the previous chapter, our awareness of our bodies impacts our awareness of spiritual realities. So too, what we do with our bodies affects our awareness of spiritual realities. We're now going to discover that our bodies can become powerful allies in practicing the presence of God and in participating in his will.

In his classic work *Celebration of Discipline*, Richard Foster details a very old way of praying he calls "palms down, palms up." With practice this exercise can be done in just about any circumstance, but in the beginning it helps to practice it during a quiet time when you can be alone.

Foster teaches that you should begin by holding your palms downward on your laps as "a symbolic indication of your desire to turn over any concerns you may have over to God."[2] Call to mind everything that is weighing on your heart and mind and give it to God. Let your downward facing palms represent letting cares and concerns fall from your grasp into the hands of the sovereign God of love who holds you in existence, moment-by-moment. Notice your breathing and envision every exhaled breath as a further release of weight in your life. As Foster notes, you may at times notice a sense of release in your hands or other parts of your body as you do this.

When you've finished this part of the prayer, Foster encourages you to turn your hands over in your lap so that your palms are facing upward "as a symbol of your desire to receive from the Lord."[3] Remain in this posture with a receptive attitude as you wait for what the Lord would like to give you. With every breath you take in, receive the fullness of Life that comes from God. Breathe in his forgiveness, direction, peace, healing, or whatever else he has for you.

It's important that you remember that it's not your job

to make anything happen. Your only task during this time is to be open to whatever the Lord has for you. Whether you experience any change or not, accept on faith that God's full Life is flowing into you and enjoy remaining aware of this fact.

The beauty of this way of praying is that, if you practice it regularly, the physical motion of holding your palms down can become anchored to letting go of anything that is inconsistent with God's heart for you. So too, the physical motion of holding your palms up can become anchored to receiving God's Life and will for you in the present moment.

Whenever you find you've begun to focus on things that are taking you away from an awareness of God's presence in the present moment or are feeling weighed down by the concerns of life, you can simply put your palms down and let it go. Whenever you find you've begun to resist God's movement in your life or are trying to acquire some element of your worth, significance, or security by idolatrous means, you can simply hold your palms up so that your body is in agreement with your intention to receive God's Life.

Standing in the Middle of Infinity

I want to forewarn readers that this next suggested exercise will take a little unpacking and may strike some readers as a bit bizarre. Yet I'm convinced many will find this mind-bending discipline helpful, as I have.

First, a little background. Over the last century science

has discovered that we live in a mind-boggling universe that is virtually infinite above us as well as below us.[4] Above us, the universe is unimaginably large and expanding at ever-increasing speeds. It contains billions upon billions of galaxies, each spanning hundreds of millions of light-years and containing hundreds of billions of stars, many of them much larger than our sun. The universe below us is equally unimaginable as we are discovering particles so tiny they could pass through light-years of solid steel before they'd likely collide with another particle.[5] There is, in fact, as much "small-reality" beneath us as there is "large-reality" above us.

In this light we can think of ourselves as situated in the middle of a virtual infinity extending beneath us into incomprehensible smallness and above us into incomprehensible vastness. To remain aware of the awesomeness of the God whose presence engulfs me, I find it helpful to sometimes remember this fact as I experience events around me.

I encourage you to try this exercise. Sit in a comfortable public place and simply observe events around you. As you do so, try to remain aware of the virtual infinity extending above and beneath you and everything you observe. Let your awareness of being situated in the middle, between the infinitely large and infinitely small, form the background against which you observe everything.

I personally find it helpful to mentally *zoom out* past innumerable gigantic galaxies as I observe things while I also mentally *zoom in* on a particular tiny segment of what I'm observing (a blade of grass or a pebble, for example), and envision a veritable universe of particles flying around inside the tiny segment. (This dual focus is not easy to attain, let alone maintain, and I've found some people actually find the exercise works better when they concentrate only on *zooming out*). I then remind myself that however far out and far down my mind may go, God is present there.

As with all other Christian mental disciplines, it's helpful to remember that this is not some sort of mental trick. To the contrary, in keeping the infinitely large and small in mind, we are simply aligning our minds with reality by including as much of reality in each observed moment as we can. We are, in essence, simply trying to observe events in their truest, fullest context.

For me, this discipline adds a new dimension to practicing the presence of God, for it helps me become aware of the incomprehensible greatness and mystery of the God whose presence engulfs me moment-by-moment. I've found it particularly helpful in empowering me to remain centered in God's peace. Our problems are only as big as the frame of reference within which we experience them. When our frame of reference is no bigger than our very small and very short lives, our problems will often seem extremely large, for the same reason an ant experiences a blade of grass like a skyscraper. When our frame of reference is the infinite above and infinite below, however, our problems become infinitely small.

One more thing needs to be said. Some have initially found that this exercise made them feel infinitely small and insignificant. After all, in the total scheme of things, our lives are almost infinitesimally small and short. To counter this feeling of insignificance, it's vital we remember that the Creator, for whom the virtual infinity of the physical world is itself microscopic, is a God of perfect love (1 John 4:8). The incomprehensible greatness of God's glory expressed in the unfathomable vastness of reality above us and unimaginable smallness and complexity of reality below us is exceeded only by the absolutely unlimited, unending, and unwavering perfection of God's love, revealed on Calvary.

As we stay awake to the infinite, therefore, we must remember that the power that holds us in existence, along with every quantum particle and every galaxy, is the love that was expressed on Calvary. The awe-inspiring vastness and smallness of created reality should be viewed as a symbolic pointer to the even more awe-inspiring magnitude and intensity of God's love.

We might say that Calvary is to God's love what the virtual infinitude of space is to God's majesty. Though we are microscopic in size next to the vastness of the universe, the Creator loves each of us as if we were the only being he created. For a God of unlimited love, size does not matter.

As you engage in the discipline of situating yourself in the middle of infinity, therefore, be sure to remain aware that you are surrounded every nanosecond by the infinite intensity of God's burning, perfect, Calvary-like love.

Chapter 4

Single-Mindedness

I never lived, I was half dead,
I was a rotting tree,
until I reached the place where I wholly,
with utter honesty,
resolved and then re-resolved
that I would find God's will
and I would do that will
though every fiber in me said no,
and I would win the battle
in my thoughts.

Frank Laubach

Ever-present and ever-loving God,
We confess that we have often been conformed to
the pattern of this world
instead of being conformed
to the image
of your Son.
Free us to be wholly yours
in this moment
and in every moment.

The Flesh–Mind-set

Unless you've taken intentional steps to change, the way you presently experience yourself and the world around you was mostly chosen *for* you, not *by* you.

Think about that. You inherited a way of interpreting the world. Your brain has been in the process of being programmed by factors outside your control from the moment you were born. Your parents, friends, culture, media, and life experiences all played a part in this programming, much of which has undoubtedly been true and beneficial, but much of which has also been untrue and unhelpful.

In all probability most of this programming involved viewing and experiencing the world as though God was not present, moment-by-moment. In other words, most of this programming gave us a mind that is "set on the flesh" and conformed "to the pattern of this world" (Romans 8:6–7; 12:2). We've been conditioned to have a "flesh–mind-set" that habitually pushes God out of our awareness moment-by-moment.

What is particularly insidious about the flesh – mindset is that it largely operates without our knowing it. Once a program is installed, it becomes part of your brain's autopilot. You don't have to think about the way you experience yourself and the world. *It just happens.*

For example, you don't have to think about the meaning of each word you're reading right now because your brain automatically associates each group of letters with a meaning, according to its programming. The brain uses this same autopilot to give meaning to *everything.*

I once knew a woman who had a terrible fear of flying — despite the fact that she knew that flying in planes was quite safe. A counselor she worked with traced this fear to its origins — an event that happened when she was about five years old. Playing in front of the television while her parents watched the news, she saw a report on a terrible plane crash. Ninety-nine kids out of a hundred wouldn't have been affected by this, but for whatever reasons this five-year-old's brain installed a program that said, "Warning: Planes are dangerous! Be afraid!"

Once installed, this program ran on autopilot for the next forty years. Whenever she thought about anything that had to do with planes, her "warning" program would get triggered and she would experience instant terror. Because the program ran on autopilot, it completely bypassed this woman's consciousness, which is why she couldn't understand why she was panicked whenever she thought of flying. Yet, this was the meaning her brain automatically ascribed to planes, and it did it with the same efficiency your brain using is right now in giving meaning to the words on this page.

There is, there must be, so much more in [God] than He can give us, because we are so sleepy and because our capacity is so pitifully small.

Frank Laubach

To the extent that the way we experience ourselves and the world is determined by our flesh–mind-set, we live as semiconscious slaves to whomever or whatever programmed us. We are conformed to "the pattern of the world," obedient subjects of what I have elsewhere called "The Matrix."[1]

Double-Mindedness

The first step toward freedom from this slavery happens when we yield to the Spirit and genuinely surrender our lives to Christ. When we do this, many wonderful things take place. For example, we are forgiven by God, given a new nature and in principle set free to enjoy God's abundant Life. But as we all know, surrendering to Christ doesn't automatically transform our flesh–mind-set. Our brain continues to operate with the same autopilot programs it inherited before we surrendered.

To the extent that we remain in bondage to the flesh – mind-set, we will not fully experience the forgiveness, new nature, and abundant Life God has given us. We will, to some extent, experience and live our lives as though we were *not* forgiven, did *not* have a new nature, and were *not* given abundant Life. So long as we remain subservient to our brainwashing in the flesh – mind-set, the way we experience ourselves and the world will be largely determined by whomever or whatever programmed us. We may sincerely have made Jesus Lord of our life, but so long as we remain in bondage to the flesh – mind-set, he won't be Lord over how we actually experience and live our life.

As we noted in chapter 2, what we consciously believe has little impact on the operation of our flesh mind. The lady who had a phobia of flying believed planes were safe, but this made no difference. Once activated, our automatic programming bypasses our conscious awareness — including all the things we consciously believe. This is why acquiring information in and of itself isn't able to bring about lasting transformation. The truest and

Our useless thoughts spoil everything. They are where mischief begins. We ought to reject such thoughts as soon as we perceive their impertinence to the matter at hand. We ought to reject them and return to our communion with God.

Brother Lawrence

most insightful information in the world won't change us so long as our moment-by-moment experience of our self and interaction with the world is dictated by our programmed flesh-mind. We'll simply become a slightly more informed slave to whomever or whatever programmed us.

This explains why a person can believe they're loved by God and yet *feel* unloved and unlovable most of the time. It's why a person can believe they're called and empowered to love people and yet sometimes react to people in hateful ways. It's why a person can believe they're called and empowered to be free of greed and yet find they habitually spend most of their money on themselves. It's why a person can believe fornication or adultery is wrong and yet repeatedly find themselves involved in premarital or extramarital sexual relations.

It's also why we can intellectually know God is present in every moment and resolve to remain mindful of his presence and yet discover we've gone all day on autopilot, failing to bring God to mind even for a moment. To the extent that we are controlled by our flesh-mind, we are living as semiconscious slaves to our past programmers, and God's presence will be habitually censored out of our awareness.

Regardless of what we believe, it's our preprogrammed flesh – mind-set that determines how we experience the world and how we live moment-by-moment — *if we allow it.* We believe in God and his Kingdom, but as slaves to our preprogrammed flesh – mind-set, most of the moments that comprise our actual life are spent thinking, feeling, and acting as though God and his Kingdom were not real.

In this state, we are "double-minded," as James puts it (James 1:8). We are like "a wave of the sea, blown and tossed by the wind" (James 1:6). We live in a contradiction between what we believe is true and what we experience as real.

There remains one single duty. It is to keep one's gaze fixed on the master one has chosen and to be constantly listening so as to understand and hear and immediately obey his will.

J.-P. de Caussade

Single-Mindedness

No amount of resolutions, sermons, Bible studies, self-help books, or conferences will rectify this situation if they just provide us with more information. There is only one thing to be done, as James says, and that is to submit ourselves to God—not just intellectually, theoretically, or abstractly, but truly. Which means, submitting ourselves in the *now*—for the only actual life we have to submit is the one we have *this moment*.

The only solution to double-mindedness, in other words, is to become single-minded—to seek the Kingdom of God first, in this moment, and in every subsequent moment. Whatever else is going on—whether we're taking a shower, engaging in a discussion, watching television, or reading a book—we must try to remain consciously anchored in the present. Whatever is going on in our environment, we must try to remain aware that one *other* thing is also going on — and it's the single most important thing in any given moment: namely, we are submerged in God's loving presence.

You do not need to forget other things nor stop your work, but invite Him to share everything you do or say or think. . . .

Frank Laubach

When we can experience all of life against the backdrop of God's ever-present love, moment-by-moment, it makes us single-minded. Every moment we remain aware of, and submitted to, God's presence becomes a Kingdom moment, for it is defined by the reign of God. When we remain awake to God's loving presence in a given moment, we allow that moment to manifest God's Life rather than the preprogramming of our flesh – mind-set.

In these moments we are defined by God rather than whomever or whatever programmed us. In these moments Christ is our *actual* Lord rather than whomever or whatever programmed us. In these moments we are truly free rather than pathetic slaves who are mindlessly "conformed to the pattern of this world."

Becoming "single-minded" doesn't mean we have only one thing on our mind. But it does mean that we strive to always include one thing on our mind, whatever else we may have on our mind. We are single-minded insofar as everything we think, feel, and do is done against the backdrop of God's ever-present love. We are single-minded not because every thought is about Christ but because every thought is taken captive to Christ.

Evaporating Garbage

As we grow in our capacity to remain single-minded moment-to-moment, we begin to wake up to how enslaved we were to our past programming and how false much of this programming was. We begin to wake up the garbage in our brain. We begin to realize just how much of our thought-life is rooted in the past and future and is focused on ourselves. If we remain awake and honest, we discover that there's more pettiness, anger, judgmentalism, carnality, greed, lust, and other "works of the flesh" in our brain than we'd like to admit.

What should we do when we discover this flesh – mind-set garbage? There are a number of strategies that are helpful in reprogramming our flesh-mind and taking every thought captive to Christ.[2] But the most important thing we need to do is simply remain single-minded. We need to view our autopilot mental garbage the same way we view all other things; that is, within the framework of God's ever-present love.

Don't judge it, hate it, get mad at it, fight it, make resolutions about it, or anything of the sort. These negative attitudes simply focus our attention on ourselves

Are you awake?

more intensely and usually end up intensifying the very thing we're judging. Whether directed toward ourselves or others, judgment always tends to lock in the thought, emotion, or activity we judge. Conversely, love that is given regardless of the negative things we see in ourselves or others always tends to liberate us and others.[3]

If your mind sometimes wanders or withdraws from the Lord, do not be upset or disquieted. Trouble and disquiet serve more to distract the mind further from God than to recollect it. The will must bring the mind back in tranquility.

Brother Lawrence

So when we become aware of our flesh–mind-set garbage, we should just calmly observe it while surrendering to the unconditional love of God that surrounds us every moment.

We mustn't imagine we have to clean up our garbage first to take it captive to Christ. The only way we can take our garbage captive to Christ is simply by submitting it, just as it is, to Christ. Aware that the love Christ expressed on Calvary envelops us at this moment, we calmly observe our mental garbage.

Watch what happens. The nonpresent, self-centered, petty, angry, judging, carnal garbage in our mind disappears. The very act of observing our autopilot programming in the light of God's love turns the autopilot off.[4] It no longer has any power to define us. Instead, we are, in that moment, defined by the love of God.

And now we are free. We are no longer the semiconscious slave to whomever or whatever programmed us. We and our flesh – mind-set programming have been brought under the loving reign of God.

Yet, as with everything else about life, this can only be done in the present moment. However free or enslaved we were in the past or will be in the future is completely irrelevant. The only thing that matters — for it's the only thing that is real — is this present moment.

EXERCISES

Observing Your Mind and Heart

One of the skills you're developing as you practice God's presence is the ability to observe your own experience. Most people go through life so completely identified with their thoughts, feelings, and urges that they are essentially slaves to them. We don't make the distinction between "this particular thought" and "me," so we just ride the waves of whatever happens to be affecting us in the moment. We think we *are* what we think and feel, moment-by-moment. To free ourselves from this kind of bondage, we're going to have to develop our ability to notice our experience in a gracious, nonjudgmental way while returning again and again to the reality of God's presence in the present moment.

[Practicing the presence] is ... the resolution to all other spiritual problems.

Brother Lawrence

Try a little experiment to see if you can experience what I'm talking about. Recall a harsh or judgmental thought that you've had recently. It might be something like "I'm so stupid" or "That person is such a jerk." Remember how it felt or how you responded when you were having that thought.

Now imagine that instead of just thinking that thought, you *observed* yourself thinking that thought. It might even be helpful to say something to yourself like, "I notice the thought that I'm stupid." And now, as you observe yourself thinking the thought that you're stupid, become aware that you're immersed in God's ever-present love. Notice what changes as you observe yourself thinking "I am stupid" while engulfed by God's perfect love. You'll find the power of the indicting thought dissipates, for you're now experiencing the truth that *you are more than your thought*. The *real* "you" is the "you" that is defined by God's love, not the indicting thought.

I encourage you to cultivate the habit of stepping outside your thought life to simply observe what is there—without judging it—while remaining mindful of God's loving presence. Using whatever reminder strategies work for you, simply make it a point to observe your thoughts and emotions with Jesus next to you throughout each day. The more you engage in this activity, the less power your automatic judgmental thoughts and feelings have in defining you.

If at any point you notice you begin to judge the judgments you're observing, just make *those* judgments part of your nonjudgmental observation. And if you notice that your mind and heart are weighted down with regrets and worries as you observe them with Jesus by your side, just put your palms down and let them fall into the sovereign hands of the always-present, all-loving God. Then turn your palms up and breathe in the fullness of Life that God graciously pours into you—even when your brain is oppressed with the judgments of the flesh–mind-set.

Doing Everything for the Lord

Lawrence, de Caussade, and Laubach each stress the importance of transforming everything we do as an act of service and worship to God. This is one of the surest ways to stay awake to God's presence and ensure that our thoughts remain captive to Christ. Indeed, Brother Lawrence found that the tedious job of washing dishes became a blessed sacrament and was profoundly fulfilling when he washed them as an act of service and praise toward God.

As you engage in any task, commit to doing it for God. It helps to vocalize your thoughts and intentions. As you carry out your task, you might say things like, "I offer this task up to you Lord" or "This present moment is all that matters, and I offer it up to you." With Brother Lawrence, you'll find that garbage in the mind tends to evaporate as you make every task an act of worship. The only way to effectively fight darkness is by flooding the mind with light.

Thinking in Terms of "We"

Laubach says that the single most important thing that helped him become habitually aware of God's presence was when he learned to transform his thinking into a conversation with Christ. "All thought employs silent words and is really conversation with your inner self," he observes. "Instead of talking to yourself," he recommends we "form the habit of talking to Christ. . . . Make all thought a conversation with the Lord."

So, for example, instead of thinking "What should I do?" Laubach suggests we think "What should *we* do?" or "What would you have me do?" Similarly, when reading a book, Laubach says you should "keep a running conversation with Him about the pages you are reading."

No aspect of our flesh – mind-set is more deeply embedded in our consciousness than our proclivity to be self-absorbed. Our fallen "I" is at the center of the universe. Cultivating the habit of thinking as a conversation with God rather than merely talking to ourselves is thus challenging, to say the least. Ask God to help you think of creative reminders. For example, before reading a book you might insert little sticky Post-it® notes throughout the book that say things like, "Remember, Jesus longs to read this book with you." With persistence, you'll find that over time thinking in terms of "we" rather than "I" gradually becomes more natural, which indicates that your very identity is being shaped in relation to God rather than merely in relation to yourself.

Chapter 5

Living in Love

An ecstasy of perfect love
pervades the fulfillment of his will
by those who surrender to it;
and this surrender
practiced each moment
embodies every kind of virtue and excellence.
Jean-Pierre de Caussade

Our ever-present Savior and Friend,
You long to pour your perfect love into us
and have your perfect love
flow through us
to all others.
Help us to remain aware of your love
and surrendered to your love
in this moment
and in every moment.

The Inadequacy of Information

Around five hundred years ago Western culture underwent what's called "the scientific revolution." At that time our culture discovered that, with the right information, the laws of nature could be harnessed to our advantage. We learned that "knowledge is power." This mind-set has produced a culture of people who put a great deal of trust in information. We tend to assume there is no problem that can't be resolved if only we acquire the right information.

This is one of the reasons why many contemporary Western Christians place so much stress on hearing sermons, engaging in Bible studies, reading books, and attending seminars and conferences. We believe that acquiring information is the key to helping us grow spiritually and solving our personal and social problems.

Of course, it can't be denied that *sometimes* information helps people grow and *sometimes* helps people solve problems. But it also can't be denied that, while knowledge may give us power in all other areas of life, it does not on its own empower us to become more Christlike. When it comes to living in the Kingdom, moment-by-moment, our typical Western confidence in information is misplaced.

Think about it. Western Christians today are massively more informed than Christians at any time in the past. Yet no one would dare to claim that we're generally more spiritually mature than Christians in the past. To the contrary, all indications are that the core values and lifestyle of most Western Christians differ very little from our pagan neighbors. Despite all our sermons, Bibles studies, books, seminars, and conferences, we are, to a large degree, spiritually dead. We don't manifest

> *We need neither art nor science for going to God. All we need is a heart resolutely determined to apply itself to nothing but Him, for His sake, and to love Him only.*
>
> Brother Lawrence

much of the uniquely beautiful Life of the Kingdom. This clearly isn't a problem created by any lack of information or a problem that can be solved by acquiring more information.

In fact, one could argue that our historically unprecedented confidence in the power of information is part of the problem. Why do so many Christians today spend more time listening to sermons or reading books than they do feeding the hungry, housing the homeless, welcoming outcasts, visiting prisoners, or engaging in other activities Jesus said should characterize Kingdom people? I suspect it's at least partly because many believe they're already *living* in the Kingdom by virtue of the fact that they're *learning about* the Kingdom. The truth is that there is no necessary connection between these two things.

Brother Lawrence, Jean-Pierre de Caussade, and Frank Laubach each minimized the value of books and study when it came to spiritual growth. For the challenge of living in the Kingdom is not about figuring it out. There's really nothing to figure out! The challenge, rather, is in *submitting* to it. The only information we need to know is that the love of God that was revealed on Calvary surrounds us at every moment and the supreme goal of our life is to surrender to it. The question then is, Will we do this?

It's a question that can only be answered with a choice. And this choice can only be made in the present moment.

I don't believe Lawrence, de Caussade, and Laubach meant to suggest that studying spiritual disciplines or theology is totally devoid of value (though on occasion they come across this way). It's just that all the information in the world is worthless if it distracts from the simplest thing in the world, which is practicing the presence of God in the present moment.

> *I have read many accounts in different books on how to go to God and how to practice the spiritual life. It seems these methods serve more to puzzle me than to help, for what I sought after was simply how to become wholly God's.*
>
> Brother Lawrence

We are not brought under the reign of God by virtue of the fact that we *know* more about it and *believe* in it. We are brought under the loving reign of God only when we are actually *submitted* to it in a given

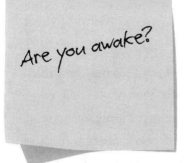
Are you awake?

moment. This submission is something we can and must do right now, regardless of how much or how little we know.

Loving Like Christ

Submitting to God in the present moment transforms us in a way no amount of knowledge can. When we submit to God in the present moment, his Life flows in us and through us. This Life frees us from the automatic programming of our flesh – mind-set and the "pattern of this world" and leads us into conformity with Jesus Christ. Relying on very little knowledge, God's love compels us to do the things Jesus did and live out the things Jesus taught. Instead of merely learning about the Kingdom, we begin to sacrifice our time, energy, and money to feed the hungry, house the homeless, welcome outcasts, and befriend prisoners. It's impossible to remain surrendered to God moment-by-moment and remain apathetic about things God is passionate about. As his Life is poured into us, it can't help but begin to be expressed through us.

Paul sums up what it looks like to manifest Kingdom Life when he tells Christians in Ephesus to "be imitators of God, as beloved children, and live in love, as Christ loved us and gave himself up for us, a fragrant offering and sacrifice to God" (Ephesians 5:1 – 2, NRSV).

We're to love others the way Jesus loved us. You

probably already knew this, didn't you? This may be so elementary you're already bored with it. Part of you may want to move onto something new and more exciting. Perhaps on

Love so insatiable as the love of God can never be satisfied until we respond to the limit.

Frank Laubach

some level you suspect your time might be better spent if we were discussing hot topics like the end times, gay marriage, abortion, open theism, church growth strategies, or something of the sort. Our addiction to information inclines us toward mentally stimulating material that requires no sacrifice of our life and makes us restless with profoundly simple material that requires everything.

It's not that any of those issues are unimportant and don't warrant healthy debate. Yet, unless we are actually surrendering to the love of God, and thus living in love moment-by-moment, these other issues must be regarded as mere distractions. We can have the gift of tongues and the ability to prophesy, and we can possess all knowledge and understand all mysteries — thus resolving all "hot" issues — yet if we aren't living in love and motivated by love, Paul says all these thing are worthless (1 Corinthians 13:1–3).

So let's not move onto something "more stimulating" but instead probe Paul's command in Ephesians 5 more deeply.

Paul tells us we are to be "imitators of God." The word for "imitate" (*mimetai*) literally means to "mimic" or "to shadow." This means we are to do exactly what we see God doing, nothing more and nothing less, just like our shadow does exactly what we do. We are to imitate God's every move, just as Jesus did (John 5:19 – 20).

Paul then fleshes out what this mimicking looks like: "Live in love.... as Christ loved us and gave himself up for us." We are to love others just as Christ loved us, dying for us on Calvary while we were yet sinners. Our culture uses the word *love* to mean a lot of different things, but the New Testament gives us a concrete picture of the kind of love God has for us and the kind of love we're to extend to others by pointing us to Jesus Christ. "This is how we know what love is," John says. "Jesus Christ laid down his life for us. And we ought to lay down our lives for one another" (1 John 3:16 TNIV). God's love always looks like Jesus Christ.

Despite the fact that we didn't deserve it, God ascribed unsurpassable worth to us by paying an unsurpassable price for us. This is the essence of love. It's not about having a nice warm feeling toward another. It's about ascribing worth to another, at cost to ourselves when necessary. So the call of all followers of Jesus is to ascribe unsurpassable worth to all others, at cost to ourselves, the way God ascribes unsurpassable worth to us, at cost to himself.

An ecstasy of perfect love pervades the fulfillment of his will by those who surrender to it; and this surrender practiced each moment embodies every kind of virtue and excellence.

J.-P. de Caussade

Loving Enemies

It's important to notice that God's love *ascribes* worth *to* us. It isn't given because God *finds* worth *in* us. Jesus didn't die on Calvary because he saw that we were worthy of it. We rather have unsurpassable worth because Jesus died for us on Calvary.

This is the most beautiful and distinctive aspect of God's love. It is unconditional. This is why it can be, and must be, extended to enemies as well as friends. When we were enemies, God sacrificially served us by dying for us, and so we are to treat all others, including our enemies. Regardless of how terrible they treat us or loved ones, Jesus says, we're to love them, bless them, pray for them, and do good to them (Luke 6:27 – 35). Even if they threaten our life or the lives of people we love (remember, Jesus and other New Testament authors were speaking to people who would soon have to face persecution, torture, and death, along with their families), we're to respond to their evil with love, serving them any way we possibly can (Matthew 5:39 – 40; Romans 12:14, 17 – 21).

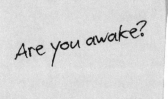

Are you awake?

Living in Love

Notice that Paul says we're to "live" (*peripato*) in this love. Manifesting Christlike love isn't something we can choose to do sometimes but not others.

It's to characterize our life moment-by-moment. As Paul says, we're to "do *everything* in love" (1 Corinthians 16:14, emphasis added). There is to be no "off" button or "choice" button when it comes to manifesting Calvary-like love. Jesus tells us we're to love others the way God causes the sun to shine and the rain to fall — indiscriminately (Matthew 5:44 – 45).

> *I choose to look at people through God, using God as my glasses, colored with His love for them.*
>
> Frank Laubach

This is the essence of what it looks like to live in the Kingdom and manifest the Life of the crucified King. It's why Paul says that *nothing* else matters except having a faith that is energized by, and characterized by, love (Galatians 5:6). All the law and the prophets hang on living in this love (Matthew 22:37 – 40).

This love fulfills the whole law (Romans 13:10; Galatians 5:14). If we live in this love, everything else we're supposed to do will be done. But if we fail to live in this love, it doesn't matter what else we manage to do; it was, from a Kingdom perspective, worthless.

Nothing could be clearer or more important to Kingdom people than this teaching. Our willingness to love like Jesus is the main way we demonstrate to the world that we're his disciples and that he was truly sent from the Father (John 13:35; 17:20 – 26). And yet it requires next to no information to carry out.

As with most things in the New Testament, the

challenge to love as Christ loved us — when we were yet
enemies — is not in *understanding* it, but in *obeying* it. Yet
obeying this all-important command isn't something we
can do at one moment and then set aside as we move on to
other, more "stimulating" issues. We can only live in love
and do everything in love, as Scripture commands, if we
never refrain from loving. The most important task of every
present moment, therefore, is to love God and one's neighbor as oneself.

Fulfilling the Impossible Command

The New Testament's command to love is not only difficult to obey, it's impossible — if we're trying to obey it on
our own power. If we're not operating out of the fullness of
Life that comes from God, everything we do — including
our noblest attempts to love — is inevitably motivated by
a desire to acquire Life. If this
is our motivation, we can't help
but "love" those who feed our
sense of worth, significance, and
security and despise those who
threaten our sense of worth, significance, and security. Operating out of our inner emptiness,
we invariably love our friends but hate our enemies. As
Jesus taught us, there is no Kingdom reward in that (Matthew 5:46 – 47).

> *We leave God to act in every-
> thing, reserving for ourselves
> only love and obedience to the
> present moment. For this is
> our eternal duty. This compel-
> ling love, steeped in silence, is
> required of every soul.*
>
> J.-P. de Caussade

Along the same lines, if we're not remaining awake to God's presence, we invariably fall back into the semiconscious bondage of our flesh–mind-set. To this extent our response to people will

be based on how our brain was programmed. In conformity with the pattern of the world, we will automatically "love" those who benefit us and hate those who threaten us.

So long as we're living out of emptiness rather than fullness and in bondage to the slumber of our flesh-mind programming, all our efforts and struggles to love as Christ loves will prove futile. We can only love others as Christ loved us if we are in fact living in Christ's love for us. Rather than focusing on ourselves and our struggle to love, therefore, we need to simply remain aware of, and submitted to, the loving presence that surrounds us at every moment.

God's Life satisfies our hunger, liberates us from our automated flesh–mind-set, and fills us with a love that freely and unconditionally overflows toward others. Only as we put off our empty old self and abide in Christ are we able to view people apart from the filter of our self-serving flesh–mind-set and perpetually hungry soul. Only now can our love for others not be conditioned by how they benefit or threaten us. Only now are we free to agree with God that every person we encounter, including our own worst enemies, was worth Christ dying for.

The challenge, then, is not first and foremost to *love* like Christ. The challenge is to *live* in Christ's love, for only then can we love as Christ loved. And as with everything else about our lives, this can only be done in each present moment.

When you're getting out of the shower in the morning and greeting your spouse, can you remain awake to Christ's love and express this love by how you think about them and interact with them?

When you're driving to work, can you abide in Christ's love and express you're agreement with God that each driver you see was worth Jesus dying for by saying a short prayer of blessing for them? Can you remain awake to Christ's love and your call to manifest it even when one of these drivers rudely cuts you off?

When we're frustrated at our overly talkative coworkers or our obnoxious, overly critical neighbor, can you remember God's ever-present love and let this love reign over all your thoughts and emotions?

When the evening news reports on a person who has committed a sick, heinous crime, will you let this trigger your fleshly programming and experience hatred toward this person? Or will you in that moment remember God's love for you when you were an enemy and extend it to this criminal?

The quality of our Kingdom Life isn't determined by how much we know or don't know. Nor is it determined by what

we did or did not do in the past. Nor is it affected by what we may or may not do in the future. It's determined by what we do, or don't do, in this moment.

Will we open ourselves up to God's ever-present love? Will we allow our thoughts, attitudes, and actions to be ruled by this love? Will we allow this moment to be a sacred Kingdom moment, or will it become just another "ordinary" moment, conformed to the pattern of this world?

Whether you're writing a book, reading a book, getting out of the shower, driving to work, dealing with coworkers, or thinking about a vicious criminal, the time to let God reign is now. The time to live in love is now.

Wake up to this present moment and you'll see it is a sacred moment.

EXERCISES

The Space between Us

Every interaction you have with another human being is pregnant with God's redemptive love and activity. Even in the darkest of interactions, God is present as a penetrating light, working to bring good out of evil. As you practice remaining aware of God's love and will permeating the space between you and others, it cannot help but transform the quality and significance of your relationships and casual encounters.

Find a way to represent God's redemptive love filling the

interpersonal space between you and others. I sometimes imagine a fine mist or soft light engulfing me and those I'm encountering. Some people envision Jesus standing between them and whoever they're encountering, touching both of them on the shoulder. With every encounter, however positive, negative, or neutral the encounter may be, ask God to reveal to you his will in the interaction. How does he want to use this interaction to impact you and the other person(s)?

If you notice judgments or anything else inconsistent with God's love rising up in your mind or heart as you interact or think about another, simply turn your palms down and release them into the hands of the sovereign, loving God. Maintain a receptive posture toward God's intentions in each present moment as you look into the eyes of this person in front of you. Notice how this changes your own thoughts and intentions.

This can be especially challenging in relationships that are difficult or even abusive. Yet, this is where the practice of God's presence can sometimes be most potent. Your job is not to *create* light in these kinds of relationships; it's rather to simply notice where God's light is already shining. How might God be using this relationship to form you? What good thing is he bringing out of this darkness?

Sometimes, in fact, God's light might lead you out of a relationship that is damaging. Even here, however, his redemptive activity is at work. Pay attention to his moment-by-moment presence and be willing to follow where he leads.

The Primary Goal of Every Social Activity

Living in love moment-by-moment is not only the most important thing followers of Jesus are called to do; it encompasses everything followers of Jesus are called to do. In this light I recommend framing every social activity primarily as an exercise in love. Whatever other goals you may have as you engage in any social activity — attending church, a party, a sports event, and so on — consciously choose to make your primary goal to love every person you encounter or think about as profoundly as possible. Challenge yourself to remain awake to the truth that each person you encounter has unsurpassable worth, not because of anything worthwhile you happen to see in them, but because their Creator thought them worth dying for.

This is, in essence, simply what it means to seek first the Kingdom of God (Matthew 6:33). Jesus certainly wasn't suggesting we seek the Kingdom first and then set this goal aside to seek other things in second or third place. Rather, we're to seek first the Kingdom of God at all times and in every circumstance. Whatever else we're doing, and whoever else we're engaging with, we are to have as our primary goal being part of the dome over which God reigns — the King's domain (Kingdom) — which means we are to be consciously submitted to him.

We are saying the exact same thing when we note Paul's teaching that we're to live in love, as Christ loved us (Ephesians 5:1 – 2). For its impossible to live submitted to the

God revealed in Jesus Christ and not love others as Christ loved us.

Silencing the Accuser

If you seriously commit to loving all people at all times, you will increasingly wake up to all the judgments that habitually take place in your programmed, idol-addicted, egocentric flesh-brain. When you become aware that you're judging someone, I encourage you to not get angry with yourself, for that is just another form of judgment. As we remarked in the previous chapter, the way to fight darkness is by turning on the light, not by conjuring up more darkness! Instead, frame your judgment as a sort of Post-it note reminder that you're not called to judge but to agree with God that every person has unsurpassable worth.

When you notice your brain passing judgment, rather than judging it and creating more darkness, thank it for reminding you to live in love. Then tell God, who is always present with you, that you agree with him that the person you were judging was worth Jesus' dying for and ask him to bless them. Over time, you'll find that you automatically remember to love and bless people as soon as you begin to judge them. And you'll likely notice that the very act of setting aside judgment frees you to experience a depth of love for otherwise unlovable people you've never had before.

Volunteering for the Worst-Sinner Award

One of the main obstacles to remaining fully surrendered to God's ever-present love toward all people and to seeing their unsurpassable worth is that we, on some level, however unconsciously, believe we are better than others. We thus think we deserve not to have to deal with them, which is why we get irritated when we have to do so. "However imperfect I may be," our thinking often goes, "I shouldn't have to waste time with people like *that*." We can never treat "the least of these" as we would treat Jesus so long as we are trapped in this presumptuous, self-serving, flesh–mind-set.

To help us out of our diabolic bondage, Jesus turns the table on us by commanding us to consider our own sin to be a large plank of wood compared to other people's sin, which is a speck of dust by comparison (Matthew 7:1 – 3). With Paul, we are instructed to confess that we are the worst of sinners for whom Jesus died (1 Timothy 1:15 – 16) — it doesn't matter how minor society or religion may consider our sin or how major they may consider another person's sin by comparison. We are commanded to volunteer ourselves for the worst-of-sinners award. Nothing frees us from our addiction to the fruit of the Tree of the Knowledge of Good and Evil — our self-serving judgments — like embracing this humble mind-set.

In this light, when you catch yourself looking down on another person, I encourage you to remind yourself that whatever sin or imperfection you think you see in another person, it is a mere speck of dust compared to the tree trunk of sin and imperfection in your own life. Yet, remember at the same time the truth that you have been completely forgiven and are engulfed in God's perfect love moment-by-moment. Out of the fullness of Life that this truth gives you, extend this same love and forgiveness to whomever you are encountering, talking about, or even just thinking about.

Chapter 6

Being Present

No moment is trivial
since each one contains
a divine kingdom,
and heavenly sustenance.

J.-P. de Caussade

Ever-present God,
You left the splendor of heaven
and became present to us
taking upon yourself our sin and pain.
Help us to follow your example
of self-sacrificial love
and remain fully present
in this moment
and in every moment.

Emily's Return

Before the eleventh grade I don't recall being interested in any topic discussed in school. I'm not exaggerating. I was about as "checked-out" as any student could be. Then in a humanities class, our teacher, Ms. King, had us watch and discuss Thornton Wilder's play *Our Town*. Something about that haunting play caught my attention, and to everyone's surprise, I actually participated in the class discussion! My contribution seemed to have impressed Ms. King because after class she took me aside and told me I should consider becoming a philosopher. I wasn't sure what a philosopher did for a living, but I felt so good about receiving a compliment from a teacher (*that* was a first) that I looked into it. Under her direction I began reading philosophy, and my brain cells started connecting (another first!). It changed the direction of my life.

To this day *Our Town* remains my favorite play. The action takes place in a small town at the turn of the twentieth century. In the play's final act, a young girl named

Emily dies giving birth, and she finds herself in the grave-
yard hanging out with other people from the town who had
died before her. There she learns that she is allowed to relive
any day of her life she chooses, though the others advise her
not to. She'll find it painful, they say, because the living
"don't understand." Emily nevertheless insists and chooses
to relive her twelfth birthday.

Initially, Emily is overwhelmed by the beauty of everything she sees. "I love you all, everything—I can't look at
everything hard enough," she exclaims. But she is saddened
as she quickly realizes that the living don't see what she sees.
Everyone is too caught up in the busyness of their life to
really look at one another. In frustration, Emily cries out to
her mother at one point: "Oh, Mama, just look at me one
minute as though you really saw me. Mama, fourteen years
have gone by . . . just for a moment now we're all together.
Mama, just for a moment we're
happy. Let's look at one another."

Sadly, her mother is too busy
to hear her.

Before long Emily can't bear it
anymore. "I can't go on," she says.
"It goes so fast. We don't have

*The present moment holds
infinite riches beyond your
wildest dreams but you will
only enjoy them to the extent
of your faith and love.*

J.-P. de Caussade

time to look at one another." And then, as she departs the
land of the living, she exclaims, "Oh, earth, you're too wonderful for anybody to realize you. Do any human beings
ever realize life while they live it? —every, every minute?"

This beautifully expresses the goal of practicing the

presence of God. It's to "realize life while [we] live it ...
every, every minute," and it includes looking hard at things
and really seeing others.

God's Body on Earth

The Christian faith is centered on the belief that in
Jesus Christ, God became a human being. This is com-
monly referred to as the doctrine of the incarnation. It
means that in Jesus, God became embodied. God left the
blessed domain of heaven and took on our humanity that we
might share in the blessedness of heaven. He took on our sin
so that we might share in his righteousness. He entered the
domain of Satan's oppressive reign to free us and transform
the world into a domain of his loving reign. Jesus is God's
loving embodiment in the world.

As the embodiment of God,
Jesus perfectly manifested what
God is like. This is why the New
Testament authors refer to Jesus
as the Word of God (John 1:1),
the image of God (Colossians
1:15), and the perfect expression
of God's very essence, supersed-
ing all previous revelations (Hebrews 1:3). It's why Jesus
could say, "Anyone who has seen me has seen the Father"
(John 14:9). Because Jesus is the embodiment of God, all of
our thinking about God must be centered upon him.

But the earliest Christians understood that the incarnation wasn't just about what God did once upon a time in Jesus. Because Jesus reveals who God really is, the incarnation tells us something about what God is always doing. While there's only one incarnate Son of God, God is always embodying himself in the world. He does this primarily by identifying with those who submit their lives to him. This is why Jesus followers are collectively referred to as "the body of Christ." We are, in a very real sense, an extension of Jesus' earthly body. We are God's hands, feet, and mouth in the world.

> *The most wonderful discovery of all is, to use the words of Paul, "Christ liveth in me." He dwells in us, walks in our minds, reaches out through our hands, speaks with our voices, if we respond to His every whisper.*
>
> Frank Laubach

Luke wrote his Gospel and the book of Acts as a two-volume work. The gospel of Luke is about the ministry of Jesus and Acts is about the ministry of the early Church. Interestingly enough, Luke opens his second volume by noting that in his "former book" he wrote about "all that Jesus *began* to do and to teach" (Acts 1:1, emphasis added). The clear implication is that his second work will be about all that Jesus *continues* to do and teach. The Gospel was about what God did through Jesus' incarnate body while Acts is about what God continues to do through Jesus' second, corporate body.

So close is the connection between Jesus and his people

that when they suffer, he suffers. When Saul (who later became the apostle Paul) was persecuting the earliest Christians, the Lord appeared to him and said, "I am Jesus, *whom you are persecuting*" (Acts 9:5, emphasis added). Paul got the point, which is why he later taught Christians that they participate in the sufferings of Jesus whenever they are persecuted (2 Corinthians 1:5–6; Philippians 3:10; Colossians 1:23).

Living Incarnationally

In the previous chapter we saw that followers of Jesus are called to imitate God in all things (Ephesians 5:1–2). We now need to see that this includes imitating his incarnational love in the sense that we are to be willing to fully enter into the life of others. We are called to live incarnationally. Jesus reveals that God is a God who is willing to set aside the blessedness of his own domain and become fully present to others. So too, we are called to be a people who are willing to set aside the comforts and conveniences of our own lives and become fully present to others. This is part of what it means to "be imitators of God" and "live in love *as Christ loved us* and gave his life for us" (Ephesians 5:1–2, emphasis added). As we live incarnationally, God himself is continuing to be embodied in the world.

Being Present on a Bus

Suppose you're riding the city bus and a woman sits down next to you. Her clothes are dirty rags, her hair is unclean and disheveled, her teeth are darkish yellow and several are missing, and she exudes an unpleasant odor. As you're enjoying reading your magazine this woman starts talking to you.

There are, of course, times when we must insist on boundaries. But in this moment you know this isn't one of them. The issue you face is that a part of you simply doesn't think this woman is worth talking to. Your self-serving flesh-mind judges this lady to be "unimportant." She can't benefit you in any way. She's not even pleasing to look at or smell. She will only take up your time.

The question is, Will you in this moment choose to die to that self-serving empty self and be present to God and to this woman? Will you *really* look at her and *really* listen to her, as much as if she was your favorite celebrity? Can you remember that this moment, with this woman, is all that matters? Can you love this "unimportant" woman the way Christ loved you and gave himself for you when you were yet an enemy? Will you live incarnationally toward her?

If you die to your old self and yield to God's love in this moment, God is not only present to you, but you become a means by which God becomes present to this woman. You are in this moment functioning as God's hands and feet and mouth in the world.

Setting Aside Judgment

As this story illustrates, one of the most common (and overlooked) things that prevents us from living incarnationally is the habitual tendency of our flesh-mind to judge. Our programmed old self sizes up everything and every one in terms of whether they will add or detract from our own sense of worth and significance. Things and people are deemed "good" or "worthwhile" when they feed us and "evil" or "worthless" when they detract from us. I believe this is why the first and most fundamental form of idolatry found in the Bible is described as eating from the forbidden "Tree of the Knowledge of Good and Evil."[1]

Every moment, and in respect of everything, [we] must ask, like St. Paul, "Lord what should I do?" Let me do everything you wish.

J.-P. de Caussade

Every one of our judgments prevents us from agreeing with God that each person we encounter has unsurpassable worth, as evidenced by the fact that Jesus died for them. Instead of ascribing worth to others, at cost to ourselves, we tend to feed our hungry souls by ascribing worth to ourselves, at cost to others. What we see when we judge another are the things we judge rather than a human being whom God was willing to die for. Our judgment prevents us from seeing their unsurpassable worth and from imitating God's incarnational love.

The New Testament has a good deal to say against the

sin of judgmentalism, for God wants us to be free to love.[2] God calls on Kingdom people to get our fullness of Life from him and die to our old, self-centered, perpetually hungry egos. He calls on us to set aside all our self-serving judgments and simply love like he loves.

Suppose a woman in your neighborhood had her husband walk out on her and is in despair. Everyone on the block knows this woman "had it coming," for it was common knowledge that she cheated on her husband, drank too much, and was a "miserable nag." Yet knowing that God didn't give you what *you* deserved, you understand you can't hold anyone else to account for what they may deserve.

While others in your neighborhood stand off in their illusory superiority, gossiping about this woman behind her back, you understand that you are called to imitate God and live incarnationally. You understand that you are called to set aside all judgment and be fully present to this distraught neighbor, taking on her pain as your own. While others look at her and see a cheating drunk and nag, you understand that you are called to *really look* at her — "every, every minute" — and see what God sees, namely, a woman of unsurpassable worth. Your choice to have compassion and befriend this woman may lead some

neighbors to distain *you*, for your loving behavior exposes the ugliness of their self-righteous posturing. But this too you regard as a small price to pay compared to what Christ did for you.

As you become fully present to this woman, God becomes fully present to her as well. The embodiment of God begun in Jesus Christ is continuing in and through you. The mustard-seed Kingdom established by the incarnation of Jesus Christ is growing — one act of mercy at a time. You are inviting the grace-filled reign of God into this painful situation and into this woman's life. Indeed, your act of embodying God's love and grace in relationship to this woman is deepening your own capacity to receive and reflect that beautiful reign of God.

Living Incarnational Moments

Of course, we aren't able to enter into everyone's life story. We are finite humans who have only limited time, resources, and emotional energy to give. It's important, therefore, that we follow the Spirit's leading to discern how, and with whom, we're to

One can pour something divine into every situation.

Frank Laubach

invest that limited time. By the same token, if we remain awake to God's ever-present love, we will find that every encounter, however trivial, becomes a sacred, incarnational moment.

The checkout clerk is ringing up the total for some

clothes you just purchased. She's done this for a hundred other people this day, but no one has *really looked* at her. For them, she was just a means by which they could acquire the items they wanted. She might just as well have been a machine. But as a follower of the incarnate Lord, you are called to live incarnationally. As God was present to others every moment in Jesus, so you are called to be present to others every moment. And as you do this, God himself is present to others through you.

So, remaining aware of God's loving presence in the *now*, you *really look* at this woman. You don't just see a store employee who is a means to an end. You see a person who is made in the image of the Creator and who possesses unsurpassable worth. Though she may be perfectly "ordinary" by cultural standards, you see a uniquely beautiful, divine work of art. You see the miracle this woman is. And so you understand that this moment, and this woman, are altogether unique and deserving of your complete attention.

Remaining mindful and surrendered in this way, you are transforming this otherwise trivial moment into a Kingdom moment, for you are allowing God to reign over it. By your intentional eye contact, your kind smile, your use of this clerk's first name (found on her name tag), your gentle conversation, and your considerate tone of voice, you are reflecting your agreement with God that this woman was worth Jesus dying for—and paying attention to. You are communicating to this woman that this casual encounter is filled with significance, for God is present, and this woman could not possibly be more significant. By your surrendered attentiveness to the presence of God, the love of God is being embodied, through you, moment-by-moment.

If we remain awake and surrendered to God's ever-present love, otherwise trivial moments become sacred, filled with eternal significance, for they are moments that embody God's love. This is how the reign of God grows in us and through us, moment-by-moment.

EXERCISES

Seeing through Jesus' "Unattractive Disguises"

Mother Teresa had a prayer she spoke each day that enabled her to minister effectively:

> *Dearest Lord, may I see you today and every day in the person of your sick, and, whilst nursing them, minister unto you. Though you hide yourself behind the unattractive disguise of the irritable, the exacting, the unreasonable, may I still recognize you, and say: "Jesus, my patient, how sweet it is to serve you."*[3]

Mother Teresa understood that when we serve others, we're serving Jesus. The trouble is that often the people we are called to serve don't look very much like what we might expect Jesus to look like. This prayer helped keep Mother Teresa oriented to the deeper reality that Jesus expressed when he said, "Truly I tell you, whatever you did for one of the least of these brothers and sisters of mine, you did for me' (Matthew 25:40 TNIV).

To acquire and retain the ability to see through Jesus' "unattractive disguises" when dealing with challenging people, many find it helpful to whisper the name "Jesus" over and over. This prayer reminds them that they are serving Jesus, regardless of how the other person may be acting toward them. Many also find it helpful to whisper a prayer similar to what Mother Teresa prayed, asking God to show them a glimpse of his presence behind the disguise of a person who is irritable, exacting, or unreasonable. Ask God to give you eyes to see the unsurpassable worth he sees in the difficult person you're interacting with. And remind yourself that, appearances notwithstanding, the person you're dealing with is for you, in this moment, the single most important person in the world. Nothing matters more than reflecting God's love to this child of God in the present moment, for the person is one for whom Jesus died, and the present moment is all that is real.

When you slip into forgetfulness, as you most certainly will at times, simply turn your palms downward and release your tendency to miss the image of God in the people around you. Then turn your palms up and breathe in God's perfect love for you and all people. With your renewed awareness, interact with the person before you as if you were interacting with Jesus himself, for in a sense, *you are.*

Imagine the Child

I find that whenever I'm thinking about or encountering a person who triggers feelings of disgust or hostility in me, it helps me envision them as the innocent child they once were. People aren't born cruel, vindictive, self-righteous, greedy, gluttonous, petty, or perverted. Life in the demonically oppressed world we live in makes people this way. Not that people don't bear some responsibility for who they become, for amid all the things that influence us, we have an element of free will. Yet only the omniscient Creator and Judge of the earth can know the extent to which each person is responsible for their actions and the extent to which they are a victim. Our job is to leave all judgment to God (Romans 12:19 – 20) and to live in love (Ephesians 5:1 – 2), which means we're called to believe the best and hope for the best regarding each and every person we come across (1 Corinthians 13:5 – 7). To relinquish all judgment and remain constant in this humble, compassionate frame of mind, I find it helpful to envision hard-to-love people as little children.

Right now, think of a person who evokes strongly negative emotions in you. It may be the child molester you read about in the paper, Osama bin Ladin or some other national enemy, or the mean-spirited boss you have to work for. Calmly observe, without judgment, your judgmental thoughts. In obedience to the command to love, turn your palms down as you exhale these judgmental thoughts and emotions. When you feel you've let go of this mind-set, turn

your palms up and breathe in God's love as you envision this
same person as a little, innocent child. Let your heart grow
in compassion toward them as you realize that something
in their history caused them to lose their innocence and
become the person you see today. Following Jesus' example,
pray for their forgiveness, for they don't know what they are
doing (Luke 23:34).

Imagine the Prequel

Most often, envisioning hard-to-love people as innocent children is sufficient to collapse our judgments and
empower us to love them and have compassion on them.
But there are other times when we may need God to actually
show us a glimpse into a person's history. Everybody has a
prequel that, if we knew it, would evoke compassion rather
than judgment on our part.

I first learned this a number of years ago after watching the news and learning about a man in our area who had
murdered a beautiful three-year-old boy. Upon investiga-
tion it turned out that this man, who was the boyfriend of
this toddler's mother, had viciously tortured this boy in
unspeakably horrific ways his entire short life. To be honest, when I first heard this report I had such a profound vis-
ceral reaction that I suspect I would have enjoyed seeing this
man tormented in hell. In obedience to Jesus, however, I did
hope and pray for this man's forgiveness.

Later that night in prayer I was given a mental picture
of a badly beaten, terrified, three-year-old boy locked in a

closet. He was begging for his "daddy" on the other side of
the closet door to let him out because he was petrified of the
dark. My heart broke and I began crying for this little boy.
Through my tears I sensed God saying to me, "Pray for
this precious, tormented child of mine." This word, which
I felt very strongly, confused me. I assumed the boy I was
envisioning in my mind was the boy who I just learned had
been murdered, and its always been my understanding that
prayer is for the living, not the dead. Why would God want
me to pray for a deceased child? Then, with unusual clarity,
I heard the Lord respond to my confusion by whispering,
"This isn't the boy who was murdered. This is my precious,
tormented child who murdered him. Pray for *him*."

Everyone has a prequel. No one with a modicum of psychological health simply wakes up one morning and decides
to torture a helpless child. What happened to this man that
transformed him from a person created in the image of God
into a child-killing monster? If he himself was viciously
abused, that would go a long way in answering this question.

While the legal system must judge this man to be unsafe
for society and lock him up, and while God will of course
hold this man accountable to whatever extent is appropriate
and necessary, my role as a non-omniscient follower of Jesus
is to simply love and pray for this precious, tormented child
of God. When I consider the man's prequel, beginning with
a time in which this damaged person was an innocent little
boy, fulfilling this role is no problem whatsoever.

Chapter 7

The Father Is Always Working

The only condition necessary
for this state of self-surrender
is the present moment in which the soul,
light as a feather,
fluid as water,
innocent as a child,
responds to every movement of grace
like a floating balloon.

J.-P. de Caussade

Ever-present Father,
you are active in everything
in everyone
in every moment,
moving the world toward the full manifestation
of your loving reign.
Help us to offer ourselves wholly up to you
to be instruments of your will
in this moment
and in every moment.

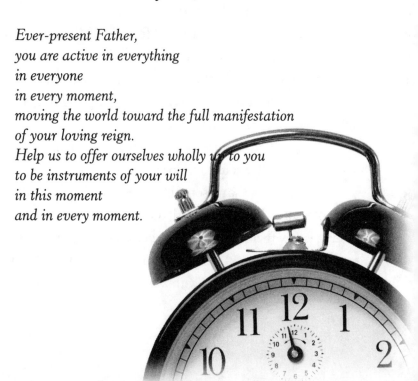

Religious Blindness

For a variety of reasons, many Jews at the time of Jesus had come to believe that heaven had been closed since the writing of the last book of the Old Testament. God was no longer active among his people. Their religion focused on holding fast to the Law God gave in the past and to various religious traditions that had evolved around it. God originally gave the Law as a means of fostering a living relationship with him, but for these people the Law had become an end in and of itself. Rather than getting Life from the God who gave them the Law, they were attempting to get Life from their obedience to the Law itself.

Religion had become a substitute for the living God.

Religion almost always does.

This is one of the reasons these Jews couldn't see that God was present in Jesus Christ. All they could see was a man who didn't follow their religious rules. For example, Jesus offended them by healing and feeding people on the Sabbath and by hanging out with people with scandalously sinful lifestyles.

They couldn't see the beautiful way this revealed a God who cares more about people than rules or reputation. Because they were trying to get Life by clinging to the past, they missed the beauty of what God was doing in the present, right in front of them.

In an attempt to help these misguided people get freed from their religious blindness, Jesus once responded to their criticism of his healing a man on the Sabbath by saying, "My Father is always at his work to this very day, and I, too, am working" (John 5:17). God hadn't stopped being active, Jesus was saying. He's *always* been about his work, and never more so than in the miracle Jesus had just performed.

It wasn't that God had stopped talking and working. These people had simply stopped listening and looking.

If we're not careful, our own religion can blind us to the ever-present God. Instead of relying on the living God to give us the worth and significance we crave, we can easily start relying on religious traditions, doctrines, and ethical rules for Life. We feel like our life is worthwhile and significant because we are right — as opposed to all those who are wrong. The more tightly we cling to our religion, the more our judgments will blind us to the living God who is always active right under our noses.

> *Divine action cleanses the universe, pervading and flowing over all creatures. Wherever they are it pursues them. It precedes them, accompanies them, follows them. We have only to allow ourselves to be borne along on its tide.*
>
> J.-P. de Caussade

Instead of rejoicing that God has just healed a man, we might find ourselves offended that one of our religious rules was broken.

Traditions, doctrines, and ethics are important. But they help us enter into Kingdom Life only to the extent that they facilitate a loving relationship with God, ourselves, and others in the present.

You are seeking God, dear sister, and he is everywhere. Everything proclaims him to you, everything reveals him to you, everything brings him to you. He is by your side, over you, around and in you. Here is his dwelling and yet you still seek him. Ah!

J.-P. de Caussade

The Father is always doing his work, which means the time to look for the Father working is now. The place to look for the Father working is here. And the people in whom we must look for the Father to be working are ourselves and whoever we happen to encounter.

The God of the Here-and-Now

Several years ago an acquaintance told me she and her husband were going to travel to Lakeland, Florida, where a "healing revival" had purportedly broken out. When I asked them if they were going because they needed healing, they replied that they just wanted to witness "God doing stuff."

I have nothing against revivals — provided they actually help people grow in their capacity to receive and manifest God's love. And I understand the natural curiosity to

Are you awake?

witness unusual occurrences. At the same time, I told this couple I was concerned with the assumption that God is "doing stuff" in one place more than another. I've known people who have spent a great deal of time and money traveling the world "chasing God" at various revivals, all the while missing what God was doing — and what God wanted to do — in and through their own lives.

The fact is, if we can't discern God's presence in our day-to-day lives, it's unlikely that we'll find him at a revival. We may find a lot of excitement, great speakers, superb music, and maybe even some "signs and wonders." But unless a person learns to find God as much in the ordinary as in the exciting, the exciting will do nothing more than serve as a momentary distraction.

Never suppose that God is more "there" than "here," or more "then" than "now." For the Father is always working — in all places, at all times, in all people. The steadfast love of God fills the entire earth (Psalm 33:15).

Your evening at home with your family may not have the fanfare of a great revival, but God is as much at work there as in any revival. And there's at least as much important Kingdom work to engage in there as in any revival. The question is, Are you remaining awake and looking for God — here and now? Are you living in love as Christ loved you and gave his life for you — here and now? For if you are, every moment becomes a marvelous opportunity to receive and express God's love. The most trivial circumstance and most insignificant moment becomes a sacred moment when we invite God into it.

It is not by considering what you are doing elsewhere that I shall become what you wish me to. It is by accepting your presence in everything.

J.-P. de Caussade

Open your eyes right now and *look*. The One who is perfect love is alive in your room, surrounding you and all others who may be present. And he is at work to bring his Kingdom into this moment. Will you remain awake and surrendered — here and now?

Practicing the Presence and Social Activism

When you consistently invite God into everyday situations, you begin to notice things you never noticed before and feel promptings of the Holy Spirit you've never felt before. Your faith becomes alive, exciting, joyful — and socially impacting.

A young mother is standing in the corner of the airport terminal, struggling to fold her baby's chair while holding her infant. No one else sees her or cares, but, since you're mindful of God's presence, you do. You respond to the Spirit's prompting and ask if you can help. In your short encounter you perceive a sadness in her eyes. As you board the plane and find your seat you whisper a prayer for this woman and her infant. In this little encounter and lingering prayer, the Kingdom is being advanced. More of God's Life has come into our dark and oppressed world. Whether or not you can see how, this woman and her infant have been touched by God's love.

A Hispanic woman is working frantically to clean tables at the far end of a busy outdoor restaurant court. No one pays her any mind — or leaves her a tip. Awake to God's presence, you notice her and respond to the Spirit's prompting to go over and greet her. Though she doesn't speak your language, your attention, smile, and kind tone communicate volumes. You're able to learn her name and thank her for the great job she's doing.

Then, responding to what you think may be a prompting of the Holy Spirit, you bless her with the last thirty dollars you have in your wallet. You know this means you will have to fast the rest of the day, but it also may mean this woman and her three children get to have supper this evening. In this little encounter, the Kingdom is being advanced. More of God's Life

> *Did those saints of old have any secret other than to become each moment of their lives God's instruments?*
>
> J.-P. de Caussade

has come into our dark and oppressed world. Whether or not you can see how, a person has again been touched by God's love.

The practice of the presence of God has sometimes been criticized for lacking a social dimension.[1] I don't think the criticism is at all warranted. True, the discipline is focused on individuals, for only individuals can choose to remain aware of, and surrendered to, God's presence. But as Lawrence, de Caussade, and Laubach all testify, when we practice God's presence we become conduits through which God's love impacts others. As we yield to the ever-present Spirit of God, we find ourselves acting like Jesus — and Jesus was a social activist. Yielded to the Father's will, moment-by-moment, he continually broke taboos, stereotypes, and laws that kept people oppressed. He had no interest in trying to acquire political power, but he took strong stands against racism, classism, poverty, sexism, and religious oppression *by how he lived.*[2] And he contin-ues to take these stands through us when we remain yielded to his Spirit, just as he was.

Are you awake?

The best thing we can do for our society and for the world, therefore, is to be as surrendered to God's will as we can pos-sibly be, moment-by-moment. People are often impressed by large political or religious rallies calling for social change, but the main way the mustard-seed Kingdom expands and transforms the world is by God's people staying awake and responding to him each moment. Rallies last a night or a weekend and are usu-ally more symbolic of what people believe should change in society than they are expressions of how people are living to bring about change in society. They create a lot of energy and may sometimes result in a few changed social policies and programs, but they usually leave people fundamentally unchanged.

By contrast, remaining aware of God's presence moment-by-moment can't help but revolutionize how we actually live. Surrendering to God's will takes us out of our self-focused flesh – mind-set and empowers us to see what God sees, love as God loves, and sacrifice for others the way God has sacrificed for us. Nothing could be as socially impacting as this.

I feel simply carried along each hour, doing my part in a plan which is far beyond myself. This sense of cooperation with God in little things is what so astonishes me, for I never have felt it this way before.

Frank Laubach

Beyond this, Jesus followers must always remain mindful of the truth that, as long as people have idolatrous hearts — seeking their worth, significance, and security in defending and advancing their self-interest or the interests of their tribe or nation — the best governmental programs and laws in the world will not fundamentally change things. Hatred, hostility, and violence are inevitable as long as people are striving to get their Life from idols rather than from God.

The best thing Jesus followers can do for the world, therefore, is to make an impact by manifesting this beautiful Life in all we do. Though Gandhi didn't consider himself a

Christian, he spoke profound truth when he taught that the best thing any human can do for fellow human beings is to "be the change you want to see in the world." When people try to fix the world before they themselves are "fixed," they inevitably contribute to the world's brokenness.

My part is to live this hour in continuous inner conversation with God and in perfect responsiveness to his will, to make this hour gloriously rich. This seems to be all I need think about.

Frank Laubach

As counterintuitive as it may seem to people who have been conditioned to place their hope in the rightness of their political opinions or their nation, the truth is that the hope of the world resides in people learning to humbly surrender to the Life of God moment-by-moment. The key to changing the world is to change our hearts and consciousness. As we are freed from our idolatry and learn how to abide in God's fullness of Life, God uses us to impact and influence others and the mustard-seed Kingdom grows (Matthew 13:31).

Responding to God's Promptings

We rarely discern the impact our Spirit-inspired, spontaneous acts of love have, but once in a while we do. A woman I know responded recently to the Spirit's prompting to call an acquaintance she hadn't seen in over a year. She discovered that just moments before she called, this woman's husband had announced that he was leaving her.

The news came out of the blue and the woman was in complete despair. This call not only gave this woman support in that crucial moment, but it eventually resulted in her discovering a Life-giving relationship with God she had never before known. Once in a while we're privileged to experience the impact our moment-by-moment obedience to God makes in the lives of others.

Several years ago a woman in my congregation saw a young man she'd never seen before lingering around in our church's gathering area after a church service. She privately prayed for him. (She was part of our prayer team that discretely prays like this for everyone after every service.) While she prayed she felt a strong prompting to give this man twenty dollars. The precise amount seemed significant to her.

> I will devote myself exclusively to the duty of the present moment to love you, to fulfill my obligations and to let your will be done.
>
> J.-P. de Caussade

So she introduced herself and simply told this young man that she felt God wanted her to give him twenty dollars. He was flabbergasted. When he told her his story, she understood why.

Because of a number of unfortunate events, this man had lost his job, been evicted from his apartment, and was now living out of his dilapidated car. For reasons he himself didn't understand, he felt like he needed to come to church that morning. (He was a believer but admitted he hadn't been to church in years.) While the collection buckets were being passed, he felt a strong impulse to put his last twenty dollars in the bucket. He tried to resist this impulse, wondering how he would eat or fill his car with gas once he was out of money. But as the bucket approached where he was sitting, he felt God say to him, "Trust me." At the last moment, he obeyed. "It was the craziest thing I'd ever done," he said.

Forty minutes later, standing outside the sanctuary, this total stranger approaches and gives him the exact amount he put in.

The Father is always working, and if we are looking for it and willing to participate, some amazing things can happen. This event let this man know that God was real and was watching out for him. It rekindled his faith and set him on a road to becoming a devoted follower of Jesus. But as is always the case, the woman who was used by God in this way was even more blessed. She experienced the profound joy of being an instrument by which God brought his Kingdom into a life-changing moment for one of his children.

To live in love as Christ loved us and gave his life for us requires that we become single-minded in seeking God's Kingdom in every moment. Aware of God's ever-present love, and surrendered to God's ever-present will, we find opportunities to be used by God in every moment.

Are you awake?

Whatever else we may see around us, we must remain mindful that "the Father is always at his work," inviting us to join him in what he is doing.

Whether you remained aware of God's presence and obeyed his promptings a year or a minute ago is completely irrelevant, as is the question of whether you will remain aware and obedient a year or a minute from now. The only thing that matters — the only thing that's real — is *right now*. Can you remain aware of God's presence and adopt an obedient stance toward his promptings right now? If so, you are no longer living in an "ordinary" moment. You are, rather, living in a sacred moment, for you are aware of, and submitted to, God's ever-present love.

EXERCISES

To get free from our bondage to the flesh – mind-set and free to be used by God, I encourage you to begin by following Laubach's example and asking the Lord throughout each day, "What would you have me do?" Remaining aware of his ever-present love, notice any prompting you sense within. If you sense something, don't overanalyze it. So long as what you feel prompted to do is consistent with love, I encourage you to act on it.

Responding to God's Will in the Moment

Frank Laubach trained himself to live in the question, What, Father, do you desire this minute? Lawrence and de Caussade stressed the urgency of listening to God moment-by-moment as well. For these authors, this is part of what it means to be fully surrendered to God. For de Caussade, this implies being "responsive to the slightest promptings from ... almost imperceptible impulses." Attuned to the present moment, all three authors encourage us to act on what our heart or intuition leads us to do. As long as we are seeking to carry out God's will, we shouldn't overanalyze our impulses. We should simply act on them.

This is a challenging teaching for modern Western Christians, for we've been strongly influenced by a secular worldview that inclines us to live as though God was not present and as though he did not want to lead us each moment. We may intellectually believe God is present and wants to lead us, but it's hard for us to actually experience this or live like this.

Not only this, but over the last hundred years we in the West have been conditioned by a naturalistic, psychotherapeutic culture that leads us to assume that everything that happens in our mind is our own doing. We're thus inclined to automatically identify all thoughts and feelings as our own and thus habitually censor out anything that doesn't line up with our own agendas. Most Western Christians aren't even aware that God is always speaking to us and trying to lead us.

We are sheep, but we rarely, if ever, actually hear the voice of our shepherd (John 10:2–16). We are his body, but we rarely, if ever, actually hear from the head (Ephesians 5:23; Colossians 1:18). We are his soldiers, but we never hear from our commanding officer (2 Timothy 2:4). Instead, we tend to live as functional atheists who are lords over our own life—despite our profession of faith that Jesus alone is Lord of our life.

To get free from this bondage to the flesh–mind-set and become free to hear and follow the Spirit's leading, I encourage you to begin by following Laubach's example and ask the Lord throughout each day, "What would you have me do?" At regular intervals face the palms of your hands toward heaven and open yourself up to whatever God may be trying to say to you in that moment. Remaining aware of his ever-present love, notice any prompting you sense within. If you sense something, don't overanalyze it. As long as what you feel prompted to do is consistent with love, act on it.

It's likely your flesh-mind will immediately object and say, "How do you *know* this is God and not just you?" I encourage you to simply observe the objection and then set it aside in order to act on your inner impression. The worst-case scenario is that you will end up performing a loving act that God didn't specifically tell you to do. This, clearly, isn't the worst thing that could happen. Conversely, if you restrain yourself from acting on an impression until you're certain its from God, it's unlikely you'll ever cultivate a sensitivity to God's voice that empowers you to obey God each moment.

Stop Over-the-Rainbow Thinking

In *The Wizard of Oz*, Dorothy thought she could find the life she dreamed of "somewhere over the rainbow." Her adventures in Oz taught her that, if she looked at things rightly, everything she really wanted she already had at home in Kansas. It's the same lesson the Scarecrow, Tin Man, and Lion had to learn. As the great seventies band America put it, "Oz never did give nothing to the Tin Man, that he didn't, didn't already have ..." (If you haven't ever noticed, the Tin Man was always tenderhearted as he went about his quest in search of a heart.)

This is also a lesson many Jesus followers need to learn. Some think God is more active over there than he is right here. Others think God was more present in the past, or hope he'll be more present in the future, than he is *right now*. Related to this, many think the quality of their life and their relationship with God would have been much better if only certain things hadn't happened in the past or weren't happening in the present. Or they imagine the quality of their life and their relationship with God will be greatly improved if only things pan out in the future.

There's no denying that God moves differently in different places and times. Nor can it be denied that past and present events help shape our life, as will events that may come to pass in the future. But the ultimate truth that trumps all these considerations is that God is as present as he ever was or ever will be, *right here and right now*. And because of this, the fullness of Life and intimacy with God you long for is available to you *right here* and *right now*, as much as any other place and any other time. In this light, looking for God in any other place than here or any other time than now amounts to nothing more than a massive distraction. You're dreaming about what's over the rainbow, in some mythical land of Oz, and this is the very thing that's keeping you from experiencing the love and joy that's all around you in Kansas.

It's time to get over our over-the-rainbow illusions and wake up to the fullness of Life that engulfs us, right here and right now. Toward this end, I encourage you to talk to God and discuss with friends ways you may be entrapped to over-the-rainbow thinking. Is there any part of you that thinks you'd find more of God if only you were in a different place or in different circumstances? Is there any part of you that thinks you'd experience more fullness of Life if only certain things hadn't happened or weren't happening? Is there any part of you that is hoping that you'll experience fullness of Life in the future, if only things go the right way?

As you wake up to these over-the-rainbow illusions, remind yourself that you are, right here and right now, engulfed in the fullness of Life that contains all you ever really need. Remaining awake to God's loving presence, turn your palms downward and release the over-the-rainbow illusions that have entrapped you. Exhale the "if only" lies that keep you from being fully centered in the present moment. When you sense you've let these go, turn your palms up and breathe in the truth that God is more-than-adequate to meet the longings of your heart and fill the emptiness of your soul. Inhale deeply God's full *Life* in the present moment.

I encourage you to engage in this exercise whenever you become aware that over-the-rainbow misconceptions are whisking you off to any place other than *where you are* and any time other than *right now*.

Conclusion

Firstfruits

All who place their trust in Jesus look forward to a day when he will return and fully establish his Kingdom. When this happens, Scripture promises, there will be no more sickness, death, hunger, natural disasters, violence, heartaches, sin, or evil. This glorious hope empowers us to be optimistic about the future, even when the state of the world gives us many reasons to be pessimistic.

At the same time, as we've learned throughout this book, followers of Jesus aren't to simply *wait* for God's Kingdom. To the contrary, our job is to manifest the Kingdom of God in the present moment. We are called to pray and live in such a way that God's will is done "on earth as it is in heaven" — right now (Matthew 6:10). As Gandhi said, we are to *be* the change we want to see in the world.

While it's indeed true that we — and all of creation — won't be completely transformed until Christ returns, its also true that we *already* have eternal life and are made participants in the divine nature. We are *already* new creations in Christ Jesus and have a new nature given to us by God's grace. We are *already* filled with God's Spirit and have overcome the Evil One. We are *already* seated with Christ in heavenly realms and blessed with every spiritual blessing.

This is why the New Testament refers to disciples as "firstfruits" of the coming Kingdom (2 Thessalonians 2:13;

James 1:18; Revelation 14:4). The "firstfruits" in ancient Israel referred to fruit that ripened and was picked before other fruit. It was offered to God as an expression of gratitude and trust that God would provide for the rest of the harvest. We who place our trust in Jesus are called God's "firstfruits" because, as a people uniquely consecrated to God, we are empowered to put on display the coming harvest ahead of time. As much as possible, we are to manifest *now* what will be true for the whole creation in the *future*.

Some day every knee will bow and every tongue will confess that Jesus is Lord. We who are God's firstfruits are not supposed to wait for this to happen. We are empowered and called to bend our knee to Christ *now*.

Some day God's perfect love and peace will characterize all of creation. We who are God's firstfruits are not supposed to wait for this to happen. We are empowered and called to manifest God's perfect love and peace *now*.

Some day there will be no more jealousy, envy, hatred, or violence in the world. We who are God's firstfruits are not supposed to wait for this to happen. We are empowered and called to purge our lives of these sorts of diabolic things *now*.

Some day all evil will be vanquished and God will be "all in all." God's glorious presence will be displayed throughout the earth, and his perfect love will define every square of creation. We who are God's firstfruits are not supposed to wait for this to happen. We are empowered and called to live in God's glorious presence in the *present* and allow God's love to define every aspect of our being *right now*.

While Jesus followers look forward to a time when all creation will be redeemed, this isn't something we're to wait for. What will be true of the whole creation in the future is already in principle true for us *right now*, and our job is to live in a way that reflects this. This is what it means to be God's consecrated firstfruits of the coming harvest.

In the Kingdom, there is no waiting. There is only *now*.
The time to be fully awake and fully alive is *now*.

The time to abide in Christ and to live passionately in love is *now*.

The time to live in God's presence and let God be "all in all" is *now*, in this moment.

And *now*, in this moment too.

And *now* . . .

Practicing the Presence and the New Age Movement

Oprah's New Age Promo

I occasionally discuss living in the moment and practicing the presence of God on my website (www.gregboyd.org). It never caused too much of a stir until two years ago when I suddenly received a half-dozen emails in the span of several days from people who were concerned I was advocating "New Age" ideas.[1]

When I looked into what was behind this sudden outburst of concern, I discovered that Oprah Winfrey had begun aggressively promoting a book called *A New Earth* by Eckhart Tolle. In this book Tolle advocates something like the practice of living in the present moment and unfortunately associates it with becoming aware of one's inner divinity and an assortment of other New Age concepts.[2] Oprah's enthusiastic promotion of his book — including hosting a two-week course with Tolle for over two million people on the internet — inspired an explosion of emails and blogs by Christians denouncing Tolle and Oprah. All of this understandably has made many Christians sensitive to any ideas that sound remotely like the material promoted in Tolle's book (and courses). They are thus worried that the practice of the presence of God reflects a New Age influence.

To dispel this concern, one need only note that the practice of the presence of God is deeply rooted in the New Testament (as I pointed out in chapter 1). On top of this, Brother Lawrence, Jean-Pierre de Caussade, and Frank Laubach all advocated the discipline of practicing the presence of God long before the New Age movement ever existed. Lawrence and de Caussade were seventeenth-century monks!

> *Practicing the presence of God is not on trial. It has already been proven by countless saints. Indeed, the spiritual giants of all ages have known it.*
>
> Frank Laubach

Yet given the enormous popularity of Tolle's work and widespread concern on the part of Christians about anything that resembles it, it seems wise to provide a brief review of the New Age concept of "living in the present moment" advocated by Tolle and show how it is radically different from the Christian practice of the presence of God espoused by Lawrence, de Caussade, and Laubach.[3]

Temporary Waves on the Eternal Ocean

Like so many other proponents of New Age ideas, Tolle advocates an Eastern worldview in which the true "you" is not the "you" that you experience as being distinct from other people. The true "you" is rather one with all reality.

To grasp this concept, imagine waves on an ocean. In the Eastern worldview, the "you" that you experience as distinct from others is one such wave. It comes into being for a moment and then passes away. But the *true* "you" is the ocean itself. It never comes into being or passes away. The "wave-you" is limited and temporary, but the "ocean-you" is unlimited and eternal. Insofar as you identify yourself with the wave instead of the ocean, you are caught in an illusion—what is referred to in Hinduism as *maya* (a Sanskrit term Tolle uses frequently).

According to Tolle and the Eastern worldview in general, every problem we have as individuals and as a race is the result of our entrapment in *maya*. We define ourselves over and against other people and other things rather than as one with all other people and all other things. We struggle with anxiety, fear, depression, anger, envy, emptiness, hatred, and violence only because we mistakenly identify ourselves with our wave-self rather than our ocean-self.

What use is the most sublime enlightenment and divine revelation if we do not love the will of God?

J.-P. de Caussade

According to Tolle, if we simply realize that our real self is the eternal ocean instead of the temporary wave, our negative emotions and behaviors will disappear. Tolle says that "the secret of all success and happiness" is found in three words: "One With Life" (115). This "Life" that is our essence is "the Source" of all things, just as the ocean is the source of all waves.

In fact, according to Tolle, our essence is nothing other than God himself, the eternal "I AM" spoken by God in the Bible (26). If we can become aware that our "true self" is God rather than this temporary human self that experiences itself as distinct from God, then, Tolle insists, we will be free. We will view our distinct individuality as a mere temporary expression of who we really are, but not as the essence of who we are. The negative emotions and behaviors that arise when we mistakenly define ourselves over and against other things will then disappear.

Our only business is to love and delight ourselves in God.

Frank Laubach

The reason Tolle advocates living in the present moment is that he believes it is the only way we can realize our "I AM" identity. When we are caught in *maya*, mistakenly identifying ourselves as a temporary wave instead of the eternal ocean, we cling to the past and future as a futile means of trying to give our limited, temporary wave-self more reality and more security. But if we can instead remain focused on the present moment, continually aware of our identity as the ocean—that is, as "Life," "the Source," or "God"—our attachment to our temporary wave-self disappears, as does all the negative emotions and behaviors that go along with this attachment.

Love or Undifferentiated Oneness?

The Eastern worldview that Tolle espouses fundamentally contradicts the biblical worldview, and it's important to understand why. If reality is ultimately one, then our experience of being distinct from God and other people is ultimately unreal. This is part of the illusion we need to wake up from if we're to experience "success and happiness." But this implies that the Bible's teaching that the central goal of life is to *love* God and other people must be mistaken, for you have to be *distinct* from another to love them. In fact, if ultimate reality is one, then the Bible's teaching that God eternally exists as the perfect love between the Father, Son, and Holy Spirit — and that God loves us as beings that he created to be distinct from himself — is incorrect.

To his credit, Tolle comes close to admitting this. The biblical teaching that "God is love," he boldly claims, "is not absolutely correct." The truth, according to Tolle, is that "God is the One Life and beyond the countless forms of life. Love implies duality: lover and beloved, subject and object. So love is the recognition of oneness in the world of duality" (106).

Tolle correctly observes that if the distinction between lover and beloved is not part of ultimate reality, then love can't be part of ultimate reality. What we call "love" is part of the world of *maya* we need to wake up from. What's *really* going on when we love, says Tolle, is that we're recognizing ourselves — our

I have had no other care but to faithfully reject every other thought in order to perform all my actions for the love of God.

Brother Lawrence

essence — in others. All "love" is ultimately *self*-love. For in the Eastern worldview, there ultimately is only one thing, and *we are all it.*

The contradiction between the Eastern worldview that Tolle advocates and the biblical worldview could not be more profound. Whereas the Bible sees love as the ultimate reality (God) and the goal of life, the Eastern worldview sees undifferentiated oneness as the ultimate reality and the goal of life.

Different Understandings of "Living in the Present Moment"

These contradictory worldviews produce contradictory understandings of what it means to live in the present moment. For Tolle and other New Age and Eastern writers whom he echoes, the purpose of staying attentive to the present moment is to realize our identity *as* God. "The wave" needs to wake up to the truth that it really is "the ocean." By contrast, for Brother Lawrence, Jean-Pierre de Caussade, and Frank Laubach, the purpose of staying attentive to the present moment is to cultivate a loving relationship *with* God. They advocate practicing the presence *of* God rather than practicing the presence *as*

> *The Love of God, submission to his divine action; that is what is necessary to sanctify souls, that is all that is required of them; and their faithfulness in responding to it is what gives them grace.*
>
> J.-P. de Caussade

God. To remain aware of God's presence presupposes that we remain aware that we are not ourselves God.

Along the same lines, while Tolle presents the practice of living in the present moment as a way of escaping the misery of self-centeredness, the practice he advocates is actually profoundly self-centered. The purpose, Tolle would argue, is to help people discover "success and happiness" by cultivating an expanded experience of themselves. Can anything be more self-centered than trying to convince yourself that you are God? From a biblical perspective, this isn't freedom from illusion; it is the most extreme bondage to illusion.

By contrast, the Christian practice of living in the present moment genuinely frees people from the misery of self-centeredness, for it is profoundly God-focused. The way to be free from the misery of self-focus isn't to try to identify oneself *as* God, but to enter into a moment-by-moment loving and surrendered relationship *with* God.

It's clear, therefore, that the Christian practice of the presence of God is anything but a borrowed concept from the New Age movement. It predates the New Age, being rooted firmly in Scripture and practiced throughout church history. And it is centered on cultivating an unbroken relationship *with* God rather than cultivating a self-absorbed awareness of oneself *as* God.

It shouldn't surprise any Jesus follower that biblical truths and traditional Christian practices are copied and distorted by non-Christians. But it should surprise us that any Jesus follower would make the tragic mistake of allowing the distorted copy to undermine their confidence in the biblical truth and traditional practice.

In this light, I emphatically encourage Kingdom people to passionately embrace the practice of the presence of God and to turn their palms down and release any fear they might have over New Age imitations.

Acknowledgments

As with so much of my work, this book would not have been possible were it not for the love, support, patience, and understanding of my loving wife and best friend, Shelley. I love my Beso!

I'm also blessed beyond measure with a group of close friends with whom I share life. For the last fifteen years we have been helping each other grow as fully alive, Jesus-loving human beings. Thank you Alex and Julie Ross, Greg and Marcia Erickson, and Dave and Terri Churchill. I love you guys!

A special thanks needs to be extended to Terri. This remarkable friend, poet, thinker, and spiritual pilgrim offered tremendous feedback on this book, especially on the Spiritual Exercises. Terri, you are a tremendous gift to me, as you are to the entire community of Abba's Kingdom.

Notes

Introduction: "Now" Is Where God Lives

1. All quotes from the writings of Brother Lawrence and Frank Laubach throughout this book are from Brother Lawrence, Frank Laubach, *Practicing His Presence*, Library of Christian Classics, Vol. I (Jacksonville, Fla.: SeedSowers, 1985). All quotes of de Caussade throughout this book are from J.-P. de Caussade, trans. Kitty Muggeridge, *The Sacrament of the Present Moment* (New York: HarperCollins, 1989).

2. A few of the books on spiritual discipleship I've found most helpful are Dallas Willard, *The Spirit of the Disciplines* (San Francisco: HarperSanFrancisco, 1988); Dallas Willard, *Renovation of the Heart* (Colorado Springs: NavPress, 2002); Richard Foster, *Celebration of Discipline* (San Francisco: HarperSanFrancisco, 1988); Ruth Haley Barton, *Sacred Rhythms* (Downers Grove, Ill.: InterVarsity, 2006); Madame Guyon, *Experiencing the Depth of Jesus Christ* (Jacksonville, Fla.: Christian Books/SeedSowers, 1975); Keri Wyatt Kent, *The Garden of the Soul* (Downers Grove, Ill.: InterVarsity, 2002); and Lee C. Camp, *Mere Discipleship* (Grand Rapids: Brazos, 2003).

Chapter 1: Mere Christianity

1. Throughout this book I will capitalize "Life" when referring to the unique quality of Life that comes only from God (as opposed to mere biological life or social life). This Life, we shall later see, is characterized by a sense of unsurpassable worth and significance.

2. C. S. Lewis, *Mere Christianity* (San Francisco: HarperOne, 2001 [1952]).

Chapter 2: Finding Home

1. For a fuller discussion on the Kingdom as participating in God's fullness of Life and the need to revolt against idolatry, see Gregory A. Boyd, *The Myth of a Christian Religion* (Grand Rapids: Zondervan, 2009), chapter 3.

2. The TNIV and some other translations unfortunately translate *sarx* as "sinful nature," which is objectionable on both exegetical and theological grounds. Exegetically, neither "sinful" nor "nature" is contained in, or suggested by, the word *sarx* (which simply means "flesh"). Theologically, the New Testament describes disciples as new creations for whom old things have passed away (2 Corinthians 5:17). We no longer have a "sinful nature." I suggest the best way to understand "the flesh" is as a false way of living. For a discussion of "the flesh" and our true identity "in Christ," see Gregory A. Boyd, *Repenting of Religion: Turning from Judgment to the Love of God* (Grand Rapids: Baker, 2004), chapter 2.

3. For an analysis of how the brain thinks and how to use it effectively to become free in Christ, see Gregory A. Boyd and Al Larson, *Escaping the Matrix: Setting the Mind Free to Experience Real Life in Christ* (Grand Rapids: Baker, 2004).

4. On imaginative prayer, see Gregory A. Boyd, *Seeing Is Believing: The Transforming Power of Imaginative Prayer* (Grand Rapids: Baker, 2004), and Brad Jersak, *Can You Hear Me: Tuning In to the God Who Speaks?* (Abbotsford, B.C.: Fresh Wind Press, 2003).

Chapter 3: Chasing the Sun

1. So, for example, Jesus and the New Testament authors consistently attribute all sickness, disease, and death to Satan, fallen powers, and demons (see Luke 13:10–16; Acts 10:38; Hebrews 2:14). Also see Gregory A. Boyd, *God at War: The Bible and Spiritual Conflict* (Downers Grove, Ill.: InterVarsity, 1997).

2. Foster, *Celebration of Discipline*, 31.

3. Ibid.

4. I say "virtually infinite" because there's no known finite terminus point at which our mind can stop in its thinking toward the largeness or the smallness of reality or in our thinking about God who, of course, encompasses both extremes. To be accurate, therefore, our thought must retain an "etc., etc." quality to it that can only be described as "not finite" [= infinite]).

5. For a "zoom-out" experience, revealing the enormity of the universe, see (http://www.youtube.com/watch?v=6rUfJG4yWLg&feature=re

lated). For a zoom-in experience, revealing the smallness of particles next to the vastness of the universe, see (http://www.youtube.com/watch?v=Sfpb9GqYLiI&feature=related).

Chapter 4: Single-Mindedness

1. For more on the robotic nature of the flesh – mind-set, how it enslaves us to a "matrix" of lies, and how we can take authority over it and be set free from phobias, addictions, and other bondages, see Boyd and Larson, *Escaping the Matrix*.
2. Discussed in Boyd and Larson, *Escaping the Matrix*.
3. For a full development of this insight, see Boyd, *Repenting of Religion*.
4. Neurological studies suggest that, even apart from an awareness of God's love and one's call to love, simply remaining attentive to one's cerebral dysfunction does a great deal to cure the dysfunction. See Jeffrey M. Schwartz and Sharon Begley, *The Mind and the Brain: Neuroplasticity and the Power of Mental Force* (New York: HarperCollins, 2002).

Chapter 6: Being Present

1. For a discussion of "the Tree of the Knowledge of Good and Evil" as referring to the sin of judging others, see Boyd, *Repenting of Religion*, 65–124.
2. See Matthew 7:1 – 5; Romans 2:1 – 4; 14:4, 10 – 13; and James 14:10 – 13.
3. Mother Teresa, "Love to Pray," *A Gift for God: Prayers and Meditations* (San Francisco: HarperOne, 1996).

Chapter 7: The Father Is Always Working

1. This criticism is discussed in Richard Foster's introduction to *The Sacrament of the Present Moment*, xxii.
2. On this see Boyd, *The Myth of a Christian Religion*. For a discussion on how the Kingdom of God is radically different from governments and nations and how it gets distorted whenever it becomes politicized or nationalized, see also Gregory A. Boyd, *The Myth of a Christian Nation* (Grand Rapids: Zondervan, 2005).

Appendix: Practicing the Presence and the New Age Movement

1. The New Age Movement refers to the rise in popularity of Eastern mystical concepts and occult ideas in the West.

2. See Eckhart Tolle, *A New Earth: Awakening to Your Life's Purpose* (New York: Plume, 2006). All page references are to this work. It's worth mentioning that, though Tolle rarely acknowledges any indebtedness to others, there's nothing in this book or his earlier work (*The Power of Now*) that hasn't been said by earlier New Age or Eastern mystical writers. For a solid, comprehensive critique of Tolle, see Richard Abanes, *A New Earth, An Old Deception: Awakening to the Dangers of Eckhart Tolle's #1 Bestseller* (Bloomington, Minn.: Bethany House, 2008).

3. To be fair, it should be acknowledged that not all non-Christian forms of meditation presuppose non-Christian metaphysical beliefs, as does Tolle's. In the Zen practice of *zazen*, for example, people are taught to simply observe in a detached manner their thoughts and feelings moment-by-moment, similar to the exercise we advocated in chapter 4.

The Myth of
a Christian Religion

Losing Your Religion for the
Beauty of a Revolution

Gregory A. Boyd, Author of
The Myth of a Christian Nation

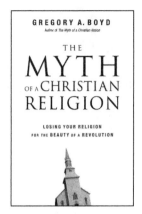

The kingdom of God is a beautiful revolution.
Marked by the radical life, love, servanthood,
and humility of Jesus, it stands in stark contrast to the values and ways
of the world.

Regrettably, many who profess to follow Christ have bought into
the world's methods, seeking to impose a sort of Christianized ethical
kingdom through politics and control. In this illuminating sequel to his
bestselling book *The Myth of a Christian Nation*, Dr. Gregory Boyd
points us to a better way — a way of seeing and living that is consistent
with the gospel of Jesus and his kingdom. Between the extremes of
passivity on the one hand and political holy war on the other lies the
radical, revolutionary path of imitating Jesus.

In twelve areas ranging from racial and social issues to steward-
ship of the planet, this book will convince and inspire you to live a
Christlike life of revolt and beauty — and it will help you attain a practical lifestyle of kingdom impact.

Available in stores and online!

The Myth of
a Christian Nation

How the Quest for Political
Power Is Destroying the Church

Gregory A. Boyd

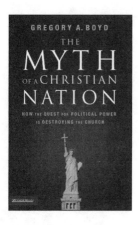

The church was established to serve the world with Christ-like love, not to rule the world. It is called to look like a corporate Jesus, dying on the cross for those who crucified him, not a religious version of Caesar. It is called to manifest the kingdom of the cross in contrast to the kingdom of the sword. Whenever the church has succeeded in gaining what most American evangelicals are now trying to get — political power — it has been disastrous both for the church and the culture. Whenever the church picks up the sword, it lays down the cross. The present activity of the religious right is destroying the heart and soul of the evangelical church and destroying its unique witness to the world. The church is to have a political voice, but we are to have it the way Jesus had it: by manifesting an alternative to the political, "power over" way of doing life. We are to transform the world by being willing to suffer for others — exercising "power under," not by getting our way in society — exercising "power over."

Available in stores and online!

ZONDERVAN®
.com